Greenhouse and Container Gardening

An Essential Guide to Building a Greenhouse and Creating Your Own Small Garden with Vegetables, Fruit, Flowers, and Herbs

Table of Contents

Part 1: Greenhouse Gardening

A Guide on How to Build a Greenhouse and Grow Vegetables, Fruit, Flowers, and Herbs in Your All-Year-Round Garden

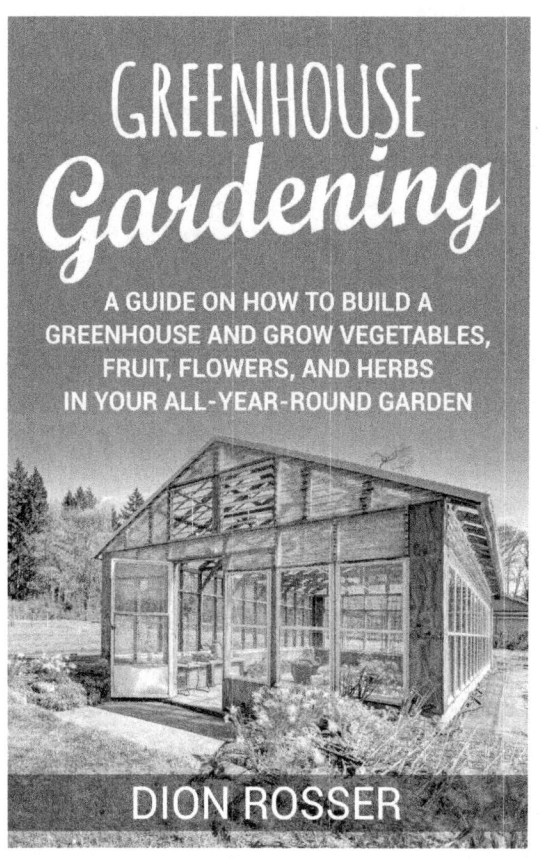

Introduction

Greenhouse gardening is a perfect way to grow food in the winter. It's also an excellent way to get kids interested in gardening and healthy. There are many different types of greenhouses that you can build, and this eBook will cover the basics of how to build your greenhouse garden with step-by-step instructions and diagrams.

The first chapter in this eBook will discuss the basics of greenhouse gardening, the definition of greenhouse gardening, a description of how it works, the pros and cons, and the best gardening tools to use in a greenhouse.

Chapter 2 discusses greenhouse foundation options such as concrete, brick, block, and cob construction; it includes step-by-step instructions for building your greenhouse's foundation.

Chapter 3 will discuss the materials and tools needed for building the frame. You'll also discover the benefits of using wood as opposed to plastic or fiberglass panels.

Chapter 4 discusses greenhouse roofing, including the different types of roof coverings and how to install them.

Chapter 5 showcases the irrigation systems suitable for greenhouses, such as hand watering, drip irrigation, overhead irrigation, and a mix of these systems.

Chapter 6 discusses the very important topic of temperature and humidity, including how to monitor them in your greenhouse.

Chapter 7 discusses ventilation and lighting, which are also very important factors in a greenhouse environment.

Chapter 8 discusses which vegetables are best suited for greenhouse gardening, several efficient bed layouts, and what pots and soils to use.

Chapter 9 discusses fruit plants that are best suited for greenhouse growing. This chapter also includes recommended pots, soil, and fertilizers.

Chapter 10 discusses herbs that are best suited for greenhouse gardening and, like the prior two chapters, includes a discussion on ways to deal with the pests encountered in this particular area of greenhouse gardening.

Chapter 11 discusses flowers that are best suited for greenhouses. This chapter includes step-by-step instructions on planting, repotting, and propagating flowers.

The final chapter is a greenhouse gardening calendar that will show you the best times to start your seeds and transplant your seedlings. It also includes suggestions for what vegetables, fruit, herbs, or flowers to plant, transplant, or harvest each month of the year.

Our goal is to provide instructions on building your greenhouse (from the foundation up), choosing the right tools and supplies for gardening, and enjoying success in growing your vegetables, fruit, herbs, and flowers in that greenhouse.

Chapter 1: Greenhouse Gardening Basics

What Is Greenhouse Gardening?

A greenhouse refers to a space with transparent walls/ceilings where plants are grown. A greenhouse doesn't necessarily have to be a house or a building. It can be a room or just a small space where sunlight can enter. Emperor Tiberius initiated the concept of the greenhouse back in the Roman Era. The greenhouse was created for the Emperor as he demanded to eat an Armenian cucumber every day. Due to this, the gardeners came up with an idea similar to that of a greenhouse to present him with a cucumber each day. However, a structure like the modern greenhouse was first seen in the 13th century in Italy.

What Is the Purpose of a Greenhouse?

A greenhouse gives you the chance to grow plants in any kind of weather. For centuries, greenhouses have enabled us to grow and eat vegetables that normally wouldn't be available due to harsh weather. A greenhouse protects the plants from extreme heat or cold and even safeguards them from pests. Now you must be wondering, "How does a greenhouse protect these plants?" The basic concept behind the greenhouse is to allow light to enter while keeping warmth trapped inside. A greenhouse reduces the normal outflow of thermal energy. It may be necessary to regulate the temperature inside a greenhouse to maintain favorable conditions for the plants in hotter areas.

People have taken up greenhouse gardening as a hobby that enables them to pass their time productively. Primarily, the purpose of a greenhouse is to extend the growing season of certain vegetables, herbs, flowers, and even fruits. A greenhouse has more benefits than we can count on all our fingers - and the best part: it's not even that expensive to make! You just need some space and tools to build it. You can build a greenhouse garden with either plastic or glass and can make it as big or as small as you want.

Types of Greenhouses

Before you begin building your greenhouse, you should recognize the needs of your plants and work out your preferences to build a greenhouse that will be best for the space you have. The type of greenhouse you will need depends on the weather conditions you live in and the sort of plants you want to grow. Here's what you will need to consider:

Temperature

Depending on the average temperatures of your locale, you will have to decide on the greenhouse structure that's best for you:

Cold Houses: *Cold houses* refer to greenhouses that do not receive any additional heat. These cold houses are specifically designed for plants that can survive in frosty temperatures, like alpines or potted bulbous plants. People typically build cold houses to extend the growing seasons; a simple cold house enables them to start growing crops earlier and extends the growing season in fall. These houses are kept warm by the sun and protect from the wind, making the inside comparatively warmer than the outside.

Cool House: A large range of plants can be grown in cool houses where the minimum temperature is kept around 45-to-50 °F. This type of greenhouse keeps the temperatures above freezing to protect the plants that cannot survive in cold, harsh weather.

The Intermediate or Warm House: The intermediate greenhouse is also called the warm house. This type of greenhouse keeps the minimum temperature at 55-to-60 °F, a temperature suitable for a wide range of plants, including orchids.

Hot House: The hothouse is also called the "stove house"; the minimum temperature is kept above 60 °F. This type of greenhouse can grow tropical plants, including anthuriums and cattleyas, as these houses are able to provide them with the supplemental heat they require.

There are many types of greenhouses – simple and complex. Some greenhouses have the technology to control the conditions, including temperature, moisture, and the water level inside the greenhouse regardless of the weather outside. Did you know that greenhouses can also be built in a way that minimizes exposure to sunlight by not having glass or plastic walls? Such greenhouses are useful in areas that have warmer climates.

Design: You can design your greenhouse any way that you like. Most of the classic greenhouses employ gothic architecture. This includes A-frame, dome, lean-to (you can even use the wall of your house or the garage against which to place this type), and Quonset-hut styles.

Materials: When it comes to choosing the material for your greenhouse, you will have plenty of options. You can find the material for your greenhouse within your budget according to your vegetation and aesthetic needs.

Framework: You can build the framework of your greenhouse with wood, iron, or plastic. Every option has its pros and cons, and you will have to choose depending on your preferences.

Coverings: You will have plenty of coverage options for your greenhouse. You can cover it with glass, plastic, acrylic, fiberglass, or double-layered polythene (which you will have to replace every two or three years). Glass is the most durable and effective option. However, it may be a little heavy on the pocket. Alternatively, plastic is a cheaper option that is also quite effective.

Environment Control

If you have the budget for it, you can gain more control over the conditions inside your greenhouse. Automatic controls may be the best option for you; however, they may get a bit pricey. You have many options when it comes to the heating system inside your greenhouse. You can use space heaters, radiant heat, a hot water system, or even soil-heating pipes underneath plants. You can implement an automatic watering system in your greenhouse if it is too large to water manually. You should consider putting a ventilation system in place for the sake of your plants' health.

What Are the Advantages and Disadvantages of a Greenhouse?

Let's take a look at some of the pros and cons of building a greenhouse so that you can consider whether it's the right choice for you or not.

https://unsplash.com/photos/low-angle-photography-of-sago-palm-vCnvm-z9fjE

Advantages

Grow Your Own Plants

One of the best parts about greenhouse gardening is that you can grow your vegetables and plants for longer periods, starting earlier than the actual season and even later than fall, as the greenhouse lets you control the environment. A greenhouse is the best choice if you reside in a cold region where growing seasons are prohibitively short. On the other hand, you can also control the environment inside of your greenhouse to make it colder if you live in tropical areas. Moreover, when you're craving a specific fruit or vegetable, all you will have to do is step out and grab it from your greenhouse!

Save Money as You Grow

A greenhouse is a cost-effective way to grow your own plants. Although you will have to bear the initial expenses of building your greenhouse, it will surely pay for itself over time. A greenhouse gives you the option of growing your own food, even out-of-season fruits, and vegetables, which helps you save money on the market prices.

Keep Out Pests

The best part about keeping a greenhouse is that it will protect your plants from the threat of pest attacks or invasion. Gardeners that like to grow vegetables and fruit are always under the threat of an attack from rabbits, raccoons, and other critters. A greenhouse protects your plants by keeping them safe from the invasion of these critters.

Starting Seeds

You can start seeds any time of year in your greenhouse, thanks to the year-long warmth and heat it offers.

Keeps You Warm

A greenhouse can help mitigate the cold winters by providing your living space with warmth and a nice view filled with beautiful plants and flowers. You can enjoy sitting in your very cozy greenhouse garden and relaxing even during the dead of winter.

Everything amazing has pitfalls as well. However, it is up to you to decide whether the pros will outweigh the cons for you. Let's take a look at the disadvantages of keeping a greenhouse.

Disadvantages

Expensive to Set Up and Maintain

Your greenhouse may have a high upfront cost. The cost that goes into building your greenhouse can exceed your expectations if not kept under control. If you want to get technology installed, prepare to spend several hundred dollars; however, the upfront cost of your greenhouse mainly depends on your preferences and the kind of greenhouse you want to make. When it comes to spending on this project, ask yourself how long it will take to get the money you invested back. Other than the cost of construction, your greenhouse will also require additional equipment, including heaters, fans, and other gardening supplies. Your utility bills may increase, depending on the interaction between your greenhouse and home.

Pest and Diseases

While the shielded environment protects the plants from getting attacked by critters and pests, it also makes them more vulnerable to disease – and certain pests. In greenhouses, pests and plant-related diseases can spread more rapidly than in an open environment. This is why you will need to stay vigilant to protect your plants from pest attacks and isolate the affected plants from the rest of the crop.

Pollination

Plants that rely on pollination through bees and birds may not get their pollination needs met. You will need to ensure that your plants receive the pollination they require, whether by tapping the flowers, shaking them, or transferring the pollen yourself from flower to flower using a paintbrush or cotton swab.

Higher Maintenance

A greenhouse is subject to marked temperature fluctuations as the day passes. Consequently, your plants may get stressed due to the fluctuations in their environment. You will have to monitor soil moisture levels as the soil inside a greenhouse tends to dry quickly. You will also have to keep checking the hydration levels of your plants and make sure that they are properly hydrated.

Space Considerations

You will have to allocate some space in your garden to build your greenhouse. Make sure that the space is big enough to cater to your plants' needs. Greenhouses can take up a lot of space, so if you don't have enough room in the backyard, you may want to reconsider this idea.

You should take some time to weigh the advantages and disadvantages before you commit to getting a greenhouse, as this can be a lot of responsibility and may even be expensive.

Best Tools to Be Used in a Greenhouse

Once you have decided to build your greenhouse garden, it is important to equip yourself with the best and handiest tools to use in the greenhouse. This will help you maintain your garden and keep it in the best shape possible. Moreover, the material, shape, size, and design of your equipment affect how well you're able to maintain your garden. Here are a few must-haves for your gardening toolkit.

Spade

Your gardening toolkit is incomplete without a spade. A spade has a long handle and a flat-edged face. It makes it easier for you to dig and makes gardening activities like transplanting, decorating lawns, etc., easier for you. You can select the shape, size, and material for your spade according to your preference.

Hand Trowel

A hand trowel is essential for every gardener as it helps with basic gardening activities, including planting, potting, and transplanting. Its handle is usually made of plastic or rubber to make it easier and more comfortable for you to hold it. Its blade should be made of stainless steel to prevent it from eroding over time.

Secateurs

Secateurs, also known as clippers or pruning shears, are what gardeners use to shape, trim, and remove dead growth from plants. It can also be used to cut thick branches, depending on the quality and capacity of its head, as well as the strength of your grip.

Fork

Forks are the dream stuff of gardeners. A good pitchfork gives them the ability to break compacted soils, aerate lawns, and create holes for seeds. Its strong fork-like body makes it easy to penetrate difficult terrains.

Gardening Gloves

Gardening gloves are just as important for gardeners as the other gardening equipment. The gloves protect your hands from thorns, dirt, and splinters caused by gardening in general and the use of rough gardening tools. Owning a good pair of gloves can make the whole process of gardening more enjoyable and comfortable for you.

Gardening Hoe

A hoe can help you with cultivating your soil and edging your lawn. It can also help you prepare beds for planting and weeding. Hoes are available in different sizes and shapes; choose one that meets your work requirements and feels right to you.

Shovel

A shovel is an essential tool when it comes to gardening. It can help you dig, loosen the soil around a plant, and move garden materials like soil, fertilizers, etc.

Wheelbarrow

Moving heavy materials around the garden can become a struggle. A wheelbarrow helps you move material around easily. It can help you move waste to garbage cans or transport any plants that need to be relocated to your garden. A wheelbarrow is a must-have for any serious gardener who needs to load and move stuff around a lot.

and Tools

It is good to have a small-handled trowel and fork as these are useful in the greenhouse.

To summarize, a greenhouse is an enclosed compartment walled with glass or plastic where plants are grown. There are many types of greenhouses, and you can choose the best one for you depending on your preferences and the needs of your plants, and the space you have available. There are four types of greenhouses: the cold house, cool house, warm house, and hothouse. There are plenty of advantages to keeping a greenhouse. However, you may need to consider a few pitfalls that come with getting a greenhouse. It is up to you to decide whether its pros outweigh the cons for you or not. The list of gardening equipment must-haves includes a spade, shovel, gardening hoe, fork, garden gloves, secateurs, wheelbarrow, and hand trowel.

Chapter 2: Building Your Greenhouse Foundation

To many people, a greenhouse may be anything from an exotic hideaway to a beautiful and practical space to grow all of their favorite plants. To some, it is a welcome space filled with lush plants and bright flowers. To others, it is a source of nourishment, where food plants are nurtured before being transplanted into the garden. Regardless of your plans for your greenhouse, knowing what you want to grow in it, the size of the space you have to fill, and how it will be used is an important first step.

Once those questions have been answered, your greenhouse foundation is as easy as laying a patio on top of a bed of perlite. It's also possible to create a permanent structure with pre-installed sliding panels secured to concrete piers. The size and shape of the space you have to fill will largely determine what kind of greenhouse foundation you need to implement. Regardless of whether your greenhouse is above ground or below, every foundation should be firm enough to erect a strong, secure structure on. With that in mind, here are some important things to consider when looking at your options.

Tools You Will Need

Before you start laying out your greenhouse foundation, you need to have a few tools on hand. Depending on your needs and the size of the project you have in mind, these tools may be as simple as a shovel and a measuring tape or as high-tech as an auger and laser measure. It all depends on what you want to accomplish with your greenhouse. Here's a list of tools you may need to complete your greenhouse foundation:

- Shovel, hoe, or spade
- Pickaxe
- Level
- Circular saw or handsaw
- Tape measure
- Chalk line
- Framing square
- Stud finder
- String and stakes (for staking out the perimeter)

- Posthole digger

- Posthole borer if you'll be digging deeper than twelve inches

In addition to these tools, you may want to have a drill with a good selection of bits on hand.

Materials You Will Need

Most local building codes will specify what kind of materials are required when working with foundations. In some cases, this information is given in an appendix; in other cases, you may find it in the foundation section of the building code. This is particularly true if your local government has adopted one of the International Codes for its foundation guidelines.

In any case, you will have two basic types of materials to consider, concrete and wood. While you can build many greenhouse foundations with either one, some types only work with one or the other. Regardless of what kind of foundation you want to build, here are your basic options for materials:

- Concrete blocks

- Brick or stone

- Hollow core door

- Pressure-treated plywood

- Treated lumber or dimensional lumber, if you will be using wood posts that won't go below the frost line.

You can use some other materials for your greenhouse foundation, including concrete piers, interlocking pavers, and more. As with anything else in construction, it's important to use materials that are rated for the job you want to do. While treated lumber works great as a greenhouse foundation, it isn't suitable if you plan on growing vegetables or other edibles in the soil. A concrete pier will support a small cold frame but is unlikely to be strong enough to hold up a larger greenhouse with multiple panes of glass.

The use of pressure-treated wood in a foundation provides several benefits. The wood is resistant to rot and insects, for starters. It also ensures that you won't have to worry about moisture getting into the wood and rotting it. Wood foundations are also much cheaper than concrete or masonry blocks, which can add up when considering the overall cost of your greenhouse. In addition, pressure-treated lumber is much lighter than concrete blocks. This means that attaching posts to an in-floor in a permanent structure will be easier because the weight isn't concentrated in one place.

Concrete construction has many benefits as well, but they aren't quite as obvious as the benefits of pressure-treated wood. One advantage is that concrete, like pressure-treated wood, is virtually impervious to rot and insects. It's also easier to clean than wooden foundations, which can be an issue in muddy areas where the greenhouse may get dirty regularly. Concrete will never bow or warp like wood does when it absorbs water and is ideal for any foundation that will see heavy use or regularly get wet.

Concrete is heavier than wood, however, and this can make putting up greenhouse structures harder. Some builders compensate for this by using metal studs to support the floor joists rather than using the concrete itself. However, depending on the size and weight of your greenhouse, this may require a bit more work than you're willing to put in. Check local planning to see if permits are required before you start.

Building the Foundation

Now that you have an idea of the materials necessary for your greenhouse foundation, it's time to build it. Before you get started, there are a few things to keep in mind. The first is that laying your foundation and constructing your greenhouse will be two separate tasks. While you want the foundation itself ready before you start building on it, small greenhouses on timber foundations can go up with just a few stakes and string to help guide construction.

Here's a step-by-step guide to building from scratch a small-to-modest greenhouse on the most expensive and labor-intensive type of small-to-modest greenhouse foundation, the concrete slab... which is also the strongest, most durable, best pest-deterring small-project foundation. Any other type of foundation for a small-to-modest-size greenhouse will be mostly a matter of basic carpentry skills, but even the finest carpenters may not be familiar with the process of pouring and finishing a concrete slab. It isn't terribly complicated, and even a first-timer should be able to produce a fine slab (of modest proportions) by adhering to the instructions on the following pages.

For the purposes of this guide, the greenhouse abuts an existing exterior wall. This is not an uncommon approach, as the existing wall provides excellent protection on one side from inclement weather.

1. Stake Out the Installation Area

Install your greenhouse foundation in a relatively flat area that gets good sunlight throughout the day. Level the soil across the entire surface of the slab site by raising or lowering its grade to strings strung taut diagonally between the corner stakes.

It's usually a good idea to have a "subbase" – a layer of gravel on the ground for your foundation to sit on. This ensures that no rocks or other sharp objects can damage the foundation once it is put in place.

For an elevated foundation, build your subbase so that it's about 2-4" higher than the surrounding area.

A 4"-6" layer of compactible gravel normally creates a stable subbase. This is especially important if you're going to use pressure-treated lumber, but it's a good idea for any foundation that will see heavy use or that needs to be well-grounded.

2. Building a Concrete Form

Having established the precise position of your foundation, build a "concrete form" along the outer edges of the subbase. Set 2-x-4 planks on edge (if pouring a 4" slab) at right angles to each other and nail them together at each corner of the subbase. This "form" defines the boundaries of the poured slab and later serves in the initial leveling method.

Once you've got your form in place, secure it to the ground using stakes near each corner. (It's going to take a lot of abuse before the

concrete is poured and finished.) You may want to measure out 4'
sections and use a line level on the inside of the form to make sure
everything is even. Ensure that the bottom of the form is flat and level and
that there's no bowing between the two pieces. You'll be filling the form to
the height of these pieces, so if one section is higher than the rest, you'll
have an uneven floor in your greenhouse.

3. Adding Reinforcements to the Concrete Area

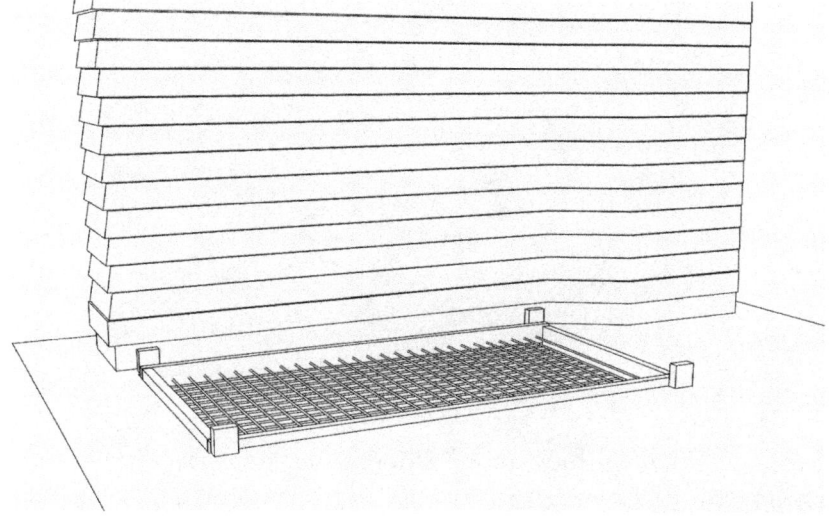

Concrete reinforcement is vital for larger greenhouses (and smaller
ones with heavy loads distributed unevenly across the floor). Cut strips of
concrete reinforcing bar ("rebar") or heavy wire mesh to fit the inside
form, and secure them with metal anchors.

Believe it or not, groundwater will travel (very slowly) through a dry,
hard concrete slab. Traditionally and typically, a 6-mil polyethylene sheet
was laid over the ground before the rebar was placed and the concrete
poured. At the time of this writing (2021), there is some controversy about
the need for and placement of vapor barriers under concrete slabs. Most
building codes still require them, at least under the living areas of a house,
though locales may vary regarding requirements and recommendations as
to the different types of vapor barriers and their positioning in the

prepping process. It will be up to you to inquire about local code, research alternate types of vapor barriers if you wish, and decide on your best course of action in this regard.

Pouring Concrete to the Form

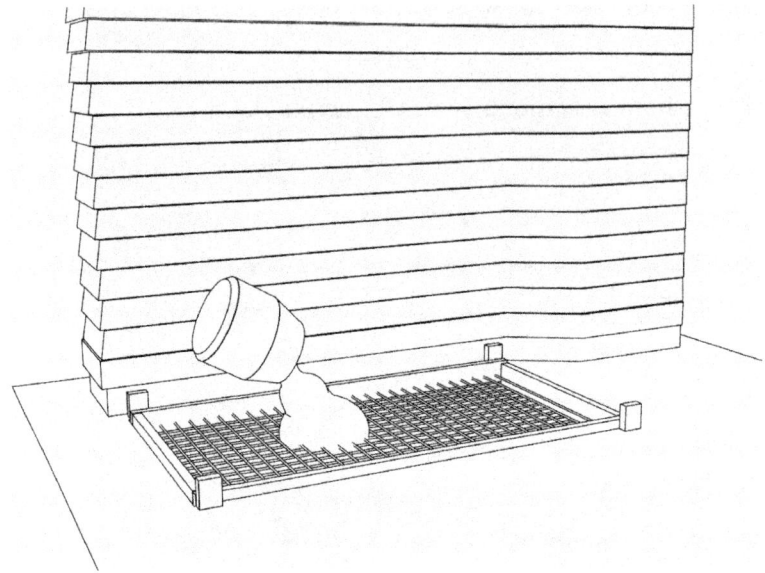

Having decided on the vapor-barrier issue, there are several methods you can use to pour concrete, but they all consist of thoroughly mixing the dry concrete with clean water and aggregate (filler material, usually gravel, which is cheaper by volume than the concrete itself) until it's about the consistency of pancake batter. This can be done in a wheelbarrow or trough using a hoe (backbreaking work, even for a small slab), using an electromechanical mixer (not so backbreaking, for small slabs), or having a concrete truck back up to the site and pour the perfect mixture at the perfect degree of wetness into the form for you. (Yes, there is a myriad of different grades and types of concrete; for a modest-sized greenhouse slab, you won't need to worry about them, and the concrete manufacturer or ready-mix supplier already knows what you need.)

Once the form is filled with the proper amount of wet concrete, the old-school practice was to "jitterbug" the slab while it was still wet. This involved donning rubber boots, wading in, and striking every square foot of the concrete rapidly, what seemed like a million times, with the bottom of a flat grate on the end of a three-foot handle, driving the aggregate down from the surface. Eventually, someone invented electromechanical devices to perform this task, and they are still available today (and still called "jitterbugs"), but the perception of the need for this initial step seems to have diminished over time.

Whether you jitterbug or not, while the concrete is still wet, you need to place a screed board (the straightest scrap 2-x-4 you can find) on edge across the long-side planks of your form and drag it from one end to the other to smooth everything out and remove any excess concrete. Doing this a few times will produce a flat, level surface on the slab, but by no means the smooth or even glassy surface that troweling can produce. (Concrete trowels are not even related to garden trowels; they're wide flat blades with handles set atop the upper plane so that they can be drawn smoothly across the face of the concrete before it hardens. They not only push down small pieces of aggregate but draw water and fine silt to the surface, making for a very smooth finish.)

If you'll settle for a more-or-less smooth finish and don't want to learn to trowel like a pro, the bull float may be your best friend. It's a large trowel of sorts on a long handle with which you can reach the center of a small slab from the edges of the form and draw the blade over the face of the concrete. If this produces a satisfactory finish for your tastes, then you have eliminated having to wait for the concrete to dry just enough that you can get out on it with kneeboards and perfect your hand-troweling technique (hurriedly, before it becomes too dry to trowel).

When the slab has dried enough that you don't leave noticeable footprints (or gouges from the edges and corners of kneeboards), sweep the concrete with a broom for a clean finish. Some old-timers do this instead of troweling, while the surface is walkable but still soft and damp, leaving a high-traction (though hard-to-clean) patterned surface.

Keep the critters and kids off the slab at least overnight; in less than twenty-four hours, it will have enough "skin" (dry, hard caking of the surface) to walk on and work on without fear of damage.

4. Setting Post anchors into the Concrete

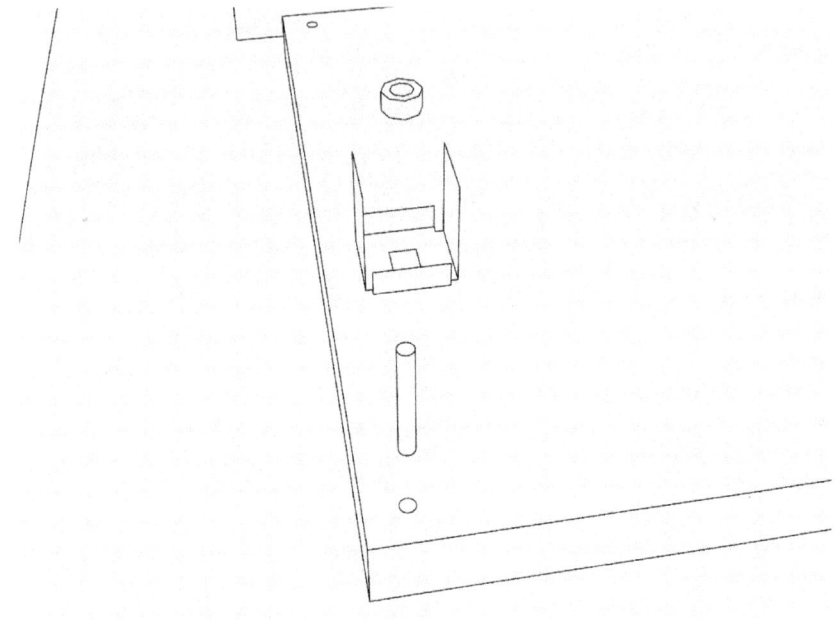

Post anchors come in various designs; some are one-piece composites of the several parts pictured above and can be simply pushed down into the concrete while it's still wet. Some, such as the one pictured, are in two or more parts because they are for setting posts on existing concrete which must be drilled first to accommodate the anchor bolt; the end result, pictured below, is fine for (hollow) metal studs that will not notice the large nut sitting at the base. Other versions entail variations on the shape shown that are pre-drilled with holes for a flathead anchor screw, side-holes for the screws fixing the post anchor to the wooden end posts, or both.

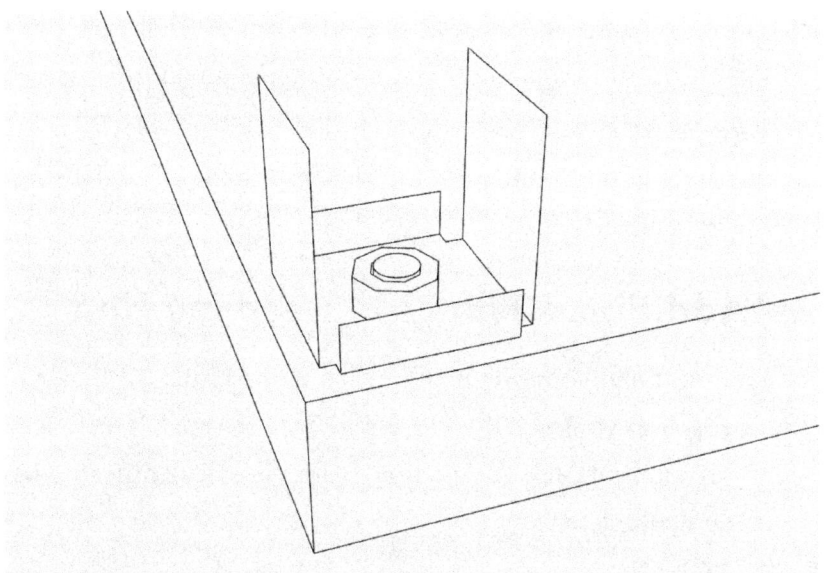

Whichever route you take, you can start assembling the greenhouse once the post anchors are in place.

Once you see that everything's lined up correctly, securely tighten all of the anchors; you don't want any wobbling or shifting.

5. Cutting the Sill Plates

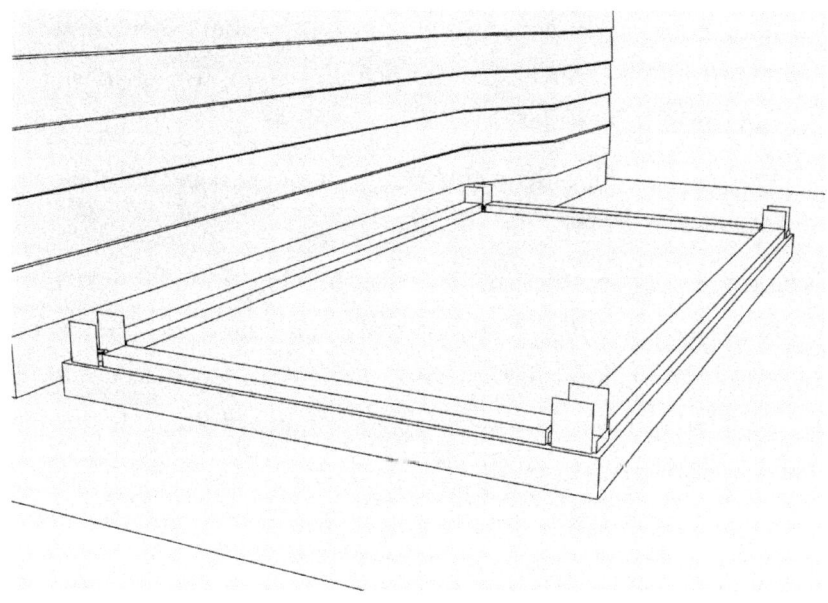

Before you bring the greenhouse pieces to your site, cut each of the sill plates (bottom board laid flat between the foundation and the bottoms of the studs) to size.

Set your greenhouse foundation together by nailing all of the sill plates in place using concrete nails.

Additional Things to Keep in Mind

1. You can build your greenhouse on a flatbed truck or trailer before moving it to your site if you have the wherewithal. This way, you'll avoid damaging the foundation before it's had time to dry and harden completely

2. If you'd like, surround your greenhouse foundation with decorative pavers.

3. Cover the concrete with landscape fabric and top it with mulch or gravel to hide the foundation and make your greenhouse look more outdoorsy and natural.

4. If you want to make your greenhouse foundation even stronger, pour concrete footers around the four corners of your structure. These footers will help prevent the greenhouse from sinking or shifting in high winds.

5. Fill your greenhouse with healthy plants and beautiful flowers to complete your greenhouse foundation.

Concrete forms are the standard for building foundations, but they aren't always ideal. If you're looking to save some time and money, build a greenhouse foundation using landscaping timbers, concrete piers, pressure-treated lumber, or a combination of any of these. It's simpler to build and less labor-intensive.

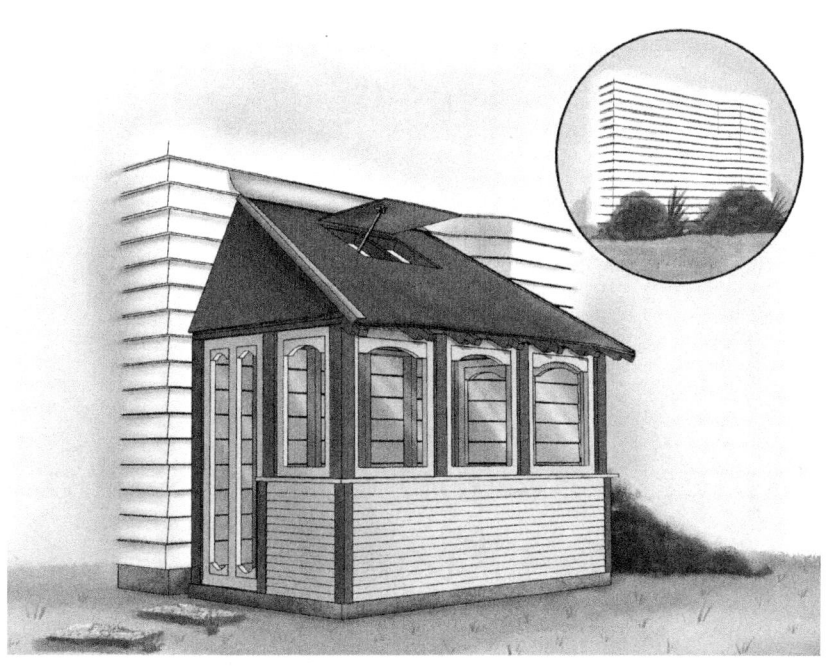

Chapter 3: Raising the Greenhouse Frame

When building a greenhouse, one of the most important things to consider is how you will build *the frame*. Many different materials can be used to construct the frame, and each one has different benefits. The material that you use can dramatically affect the efficiency of your greenhouse.

In this chapter, you'll learn everything you need to know about constructing the greenhouse frame. We'll also discuss the different materials that can be used to build a greenhouse frame and the benefits of each.

Materials and Tools Needed to Build a Frame

Greenhouses can be quite simple and highly efficient if the right materials are used to build the frame. There are several options available when building your greenhouse frame, but wood is one of the best materials. It is lightweight, relatively inexpensive, recyclable, and strong enough to support the weight of the greenhouse structure and its contents. If you decide to use wood for your greenhouse frame, then you will need the following materials and tools:

Plywood: This type of wood consists of thin sheets glued in layers to achieve various thicknesses, predominately ¼", ½," and ¾."

2-x-4: These all-purpose boards are commonly found in eight-foot lengths, but any lumber depot worth its salt will carry them in twelve-foot and fourteen-foot lengths as well. Choose a length long enough to reach from each support post to the next.

Wood Screws: Besides the obvious question of length and gauge (thread width), the material and head type of screws chosen for your greenhouse must also be considered. For joining 2-x-4s face-to-face, the standard 2.5", 8-gauge, or 9-gauge does the trick; for joining 2-x-4s face-to-end, use a 3-to-3.25" screw to carry deeper into the end of the adjoining board.

In a humid environment like a greenhouse, screws of better material such as coated copper or steel will hold up longer. Deck screws are usually made of these materials and have larger heads and deeper threads, which enhance their load-bearing capacity.

Philips-head screwdrivers and bits have become as common as the original slot-head version; however, scrounging through your toolbox for the right Torx (star-shaped) screwdriver/bit or the right wrench/socket for a hexagonal-headed lag bolt can become a pain after a while. Philips head screws are preferable to ordinary slotted screws because a little extra torque is less likely to strip the screw head. For particularly heavy-duty load-bearing applications, it may be advisable to use these instead of ordinary screws; if so, have the proper drivers set aside for that part of the construction.

Nails: Fast and strong, the good old-fashioned nail still serves on the front lines of heavy construction. Stress, however, particularly in the form of shear forces, can turn the satisfaction to dismay over time, or even quite suddenly in a windstorm; this is why wooden sea-going vessels are generally built using screws, not nails. If your greenhouse is to be situated in a place prone to high winds, earth tremors, or other sources of shear forces acting on the frame, opt for screws.

Shovels: For digging holes to anchor the posts into the ground.

Hinge-plates: Any type of pre-formed metal plate used to attach or reinforce corners, seams, or joints.

Clamps: These are used to secure pieces of wood together while you're working on them. They work similarly to a vise but are portable.

Circular Saw: A "skill saw" is used to cut the wood to the proper length quickly.

Raising the Frame

Once you have chosen the material to build your greenhouse frame, it's time to get started. To illustrate this short guide to that process, we will use the example of a greenhouse being framed entirely with wood (atop the concrete slab we built in the last chapter) and placed next to an exterior wall.

1. Tacking the Posts

Before placing the frame around the posts, you must first secure the posts in place using nails, screws, post anchors, and/or angle brackets. Deck screws are a good choice because they are long enough and strong enough, assuming you use at least two per joint. If using post anchors or angle brackets, make sure their edges are perfectly flush with the posts' as you use the drill/driver to screw them in place. The posts must rest cleanly on top of the footplate or foundation, and they must also be perfectly plumb.

2. Fixing the Center Post

Once you have secured all of your corner posts in place, then it is time to fix the center post for the door frame. The frame must be perfectly vertical for the door to behave properly; use a spirit level to ensure this, recutting or shimming the bottom of the post to insure it is perfectly plumb.

3. Installing Studs

"Studs" are vertical planks, usually 2-x-4s, that frame in the interior walls; they may be smaller in width and depth than the corner posts, and they rarely require anchor posts or brackets but can be simply "toe-nailed" or screwed in place. The studs should be spaced 16" o.c. ("off-center," meaning from the centerline of one board to the centerline of the next. Note that this is a precise way of spacing, as a measurement between the facing planes of the same two boards *may not* yield the same result because one or both of the boards are bowed, warped, or have surface imperfections.)

Spacing the Knee Wall Studs

Once you have installed the wall studs, it is time to install the knee-wall studs. Knee-wall studs are short studs set between the corner-posts; they are not load-bearing to any significant degree and may be spaced 24" apart (24" o.c.). Again, get them as close to plumb (vertical) as possible, using a level, and cut them carefully to the exact same lengths, as a sill board will be placed along the horizontal plane of their upper ends.

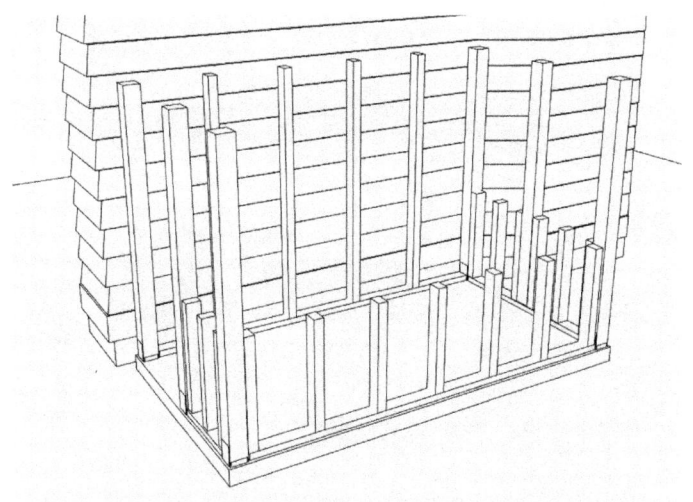

Confident that the tops of all your knee-wall studs are at precisely the same height, you can begin to tie this box together! Cut and place the knee-wall cap plates atop your knee-wall studs and attach them with 2-and-1/2" wood screws. Fix the ends of the cap plates to the end-posts with deck screws of a length commensurate with the dimensions of your end-posts (e.g., 4-and-1/4" deck screws if you used 4-x-4 end posts.) It may be helpful to drill guide holes in the end-posts to facilitate this; use a drill bit markedly smaller than the gauge of your screws but long enough to give them a long straight start.

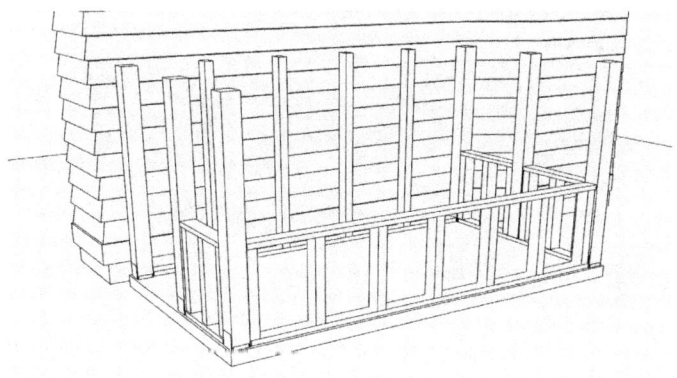

4. Placing the Walls' Cap Plates

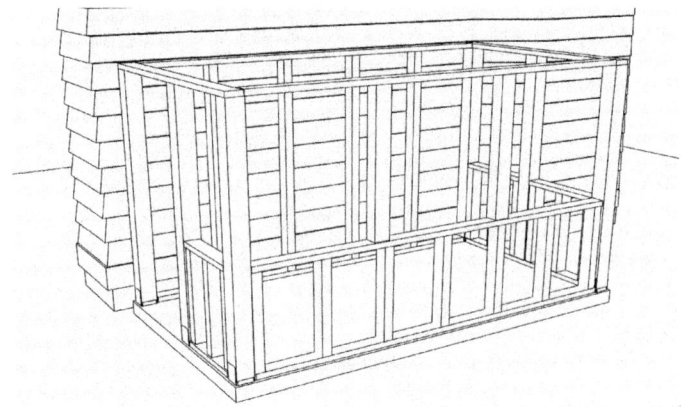

Once you have installed all of your knee wall studs, cut and place the walls' cap plates in the same manner. Countersink the screws going through the cap plates into the tops of the studs so they do not stick out and obstruct things – there will be rafters and soffit-boards going into this area later, and you want a clean, even working space here.

5. Constructing and Attaching the Roof-Ridge Support Wall

Once you have installed the wall cap plates, start building the roof-ridge support wall. This special wall will act as internal support for your roof; it is essentially a 2-x-4 atop one long-side wall, as illustrated above.

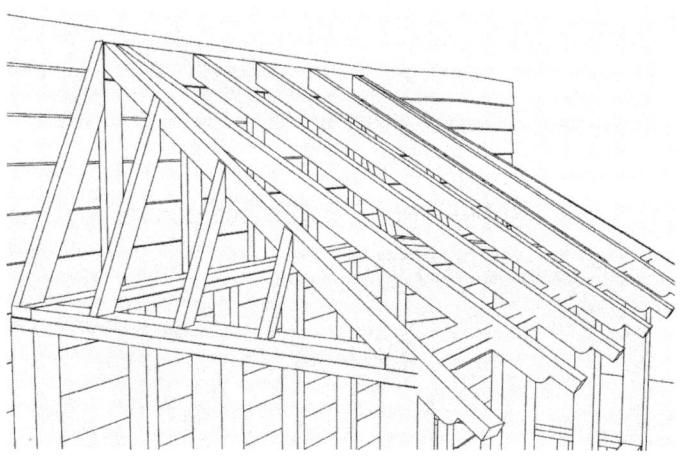

You can now start to install the rafters that will be attached to the top of your roof-ridge support wall. The angle, 45 degrees, of these rafters from the ridge beam to cap plates makes the math for their measurement and cutting much easier. The angled ends against the ridge pole will be cut at a regulation 45°. If you look at the structure from the side, you'll see each rafter becomes the hypotenuse (longest side) of a right triangle.

Installing the Corner Rafters

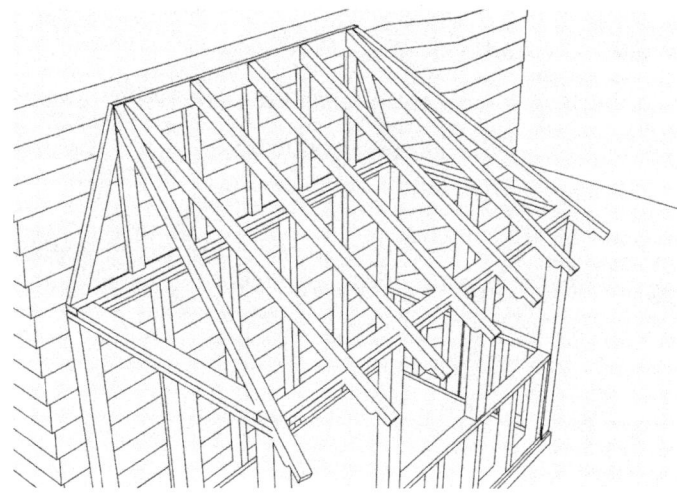

You can now measure from the corner rafters to the end walls. This is an important measurement in which you must be exact. Make sure you have a tape measure handy. This length will help you find the lengths for the side rafters in the hip wall configuration. It is also a good idea to use a spirit level (bubble level) for this. You will need to cut your trusses so that the bottom of them lines up with the top of the end wall studs. The corner rafters can now be cut at 45 degrees to make them fit properly. This is important as the roof will not fit correctly if this step is not done correctly.

6. Adding Intermediate 4x4 Posts

You now need to add the 4x4 posts that will be used as intermediate supports. These posts should be cut and installed between sills and the undersides of the doubled cap plates. These posts can be bolted to the sill plates. Use a spirit level to ensure that they are perfectly vertical so the roof will not have gaps. The posts should be fixed to the sill plates using screws and then fixed through the post into the cap plate with a larger screw. (These posts will also have a ridge beam built off them that goes across the hip walls to support your roof.) Cut knee wall sheathing panels from exterior plywood and attach the panels to the knee wall studs with deck screws.

7. Installing Siding on Knee Wall

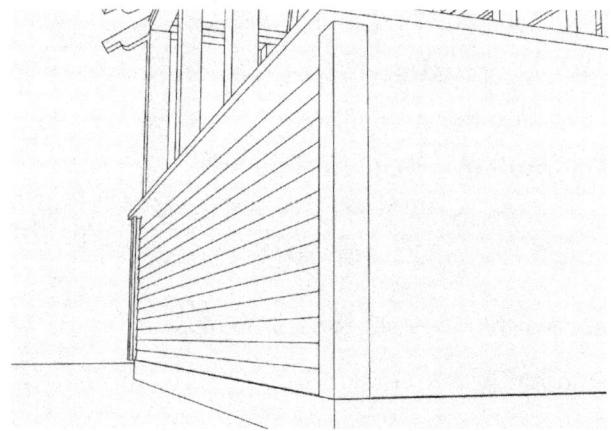

You should now install the exterior plywood siding on the knee walls (lower walls below window openings) with the front edge flush with your roof sheathing. If you are using corrugated metal siding, you can install it in the same way. Just make sure that each piece of siding is flush with the top of your ridge beam and at a right angle to the knee wall studs. You can use trim boards for this that have the same dimensions as the plywood siding. These trim boards should either be installed horizontally or vertically, depending on your preference. You can use screws to attach these trim boards to the knee wall studs.

8. Painting the Structure

Now all you have to do is paint your greenhouse frame. You can use exterior paint that can withstand moisture.

And you should consider applying an exterior stain for color. You should also make sure that you allow your paint or stain to dry completely before continuing with the rest of the build.

FAQ

- **What are other greenhouse frame designs?**

You could also use different designs for your greenhouse, including a lean-to design with a single end wall and a design with three end walls. Both of these designs only require one ridge support wall instead of two, and they will be easier to build because you will not need to create hip walls.

- **Do I need an engineer for this design?**

If you are building a greenhouse more than 10 feet wide, you should hire a professional engineer to review your plans and ensure that they meet code requirements.

- **Can I build this greenhouse in the winter?**

You should never try to build a greenhouse when the ground is frozen. It is best to wait for warmer spring weather to begin the project.

- **Do I need to use pressure-treated lumber for this project?**

It is not necessary to use pressure-treated lumber for this greenhouse build. You can use untreated wood that will be clear of knots.

- **What are the disadvantages of using this design?**

The biggest potential issue is that the frame will not be completely square, which means you need to measure and cut all of your pieces carefully.

Building a greenhouse frame out of wood is not difficult. All it takes is some basic building knowledge and the right tools to get started. This chapter has given you a complete design that you can use to build your greenhouse frame, and this design can be modified however you see fit. With a few slight modifications, it is possible to turn this design into a larger greenhouse that fits your needs perfectly. If you follow the steps in this chapter one at a time, you should have a basic greenhouse frame to be proud of.

Chapter 4: Installing the Roof, Windows, and Doors

Choosing the right greenhouse can be overwhelming, but one of the most important decisions you have to make is how to install the roof, windows, and doors. There are a few things to consider when deciding which method will work best for you, your greenhouse, and your local climate. In this chapter, we'll go over the most popular options for installing a roof, windows, and doors on your greenhouse. The step-by-step instructions will help you make the decision that will work best for you. This chapter also tackles the most frequently asked questions about installing these components.

Window Openers, Roof Panels, and Doors

Window openers give you the ability to open your greenhouse's windows for ventilation. They are especially useful during the winter when it is too cold for ventilation. You can find window openers in many different styles and sizes, so you will need to choose one that fits your greenhouse's windows. Some window openers are made specifically to hook into a certain window's lock, while others come with their locks and can be attached to almost any window.

When you're trying to decide which type of roof panels or door is right for your greenhouse, you'll need to consider the material, thickness, and possibly insulation. There are benefits and downsides to each, so it's important to weigh your options before making the final decision. It's not always necessary, but some people like to add insulation to their greenhouse. With insulation, you can regulate the temperature better and save on heating costs. Frequently, insulation is used in conjunction with double-glazed or triple-glazed glass. If you decide to install insulation, be sure to get it professionally installed.

The most common roof panels are made from polycarbonate or fiberglass. Polycarbonate is more expensive than fiberglass, but it's stronger, lighter, and won't crack or fade easily. Fiberglass is a cheaper option, but it's thicker and heavier than polycarbonate, making it more difficult to install. Fiberglass doesn't handle temperature changes as well as polycarbonate, so it can be prone to cracking.

Polycarbonate comes in many different thicknesses, and it can be cut to the exact size needed for your greenhouse. Polycarbonate is also good for withstanding temperature changes, so it's less likely to crack or break if exposed to extreme heat or cold. One downside to polycarbonate is that it can be expensive. However, if you're concerned about insulation, this material is a good choice because it's stronger and more durable than fiberglass.

Fiberglass is made of glass and comes in many different thicknesses. This material is a good option for a greenhouse with double-glazed windows because it won't shatter easily like polycarbonate. It's also cheap, so you can easily replace it if it cracks or breaks. Fiberglass is good for withstanding temperature changes, but it can be difficult to install because it's thicker and heavier than polycarbonate. It's also more likely to crack when exposed to extreme heat or cold.

You'll also need to consider the size and shape of your greenhouse when deciding what type of roof panels or doors to add to your greenhouse. If you have a glass roof, the different types of glass available will change how much sunlight enters the greenhouse, so choose carefully. It's important to get the right type of glass for your roof because it will affect whether or not you decide to add insulation.

The most common door materials are wood and glass. They're both good options for a greenhouse, but it's important to know the differences between them so you can choose which is best. Wood doors are strong, durable, and aesthetically pleasing. They also offer good insulation, but they're only effective if the greenhouse is well insulated and airtight. This means you should take extra precautions to ensure your greenhouse isn't drafty.

Glass doors are good for people who want to get maximum sunlight in their greenhouse. They don't have good insulation, so they're only effective in a greenhouse with insulated walls. On the bright side, glass doors are aesthetically pleasing, and they don't need to be painted or stained, which means you won't have to replace them as often.

Installing the Roof, Windows, and Doors

Once you've decided on the type of roof panels or doors to use, it's time to start installing them. The size and shape of your greenhouse will determine what type and how many panels you'll need.

Before installing the roof panels, make sure you have a sturdy frame. If you have a slanted roof, shingle the panels together to ensure they stay in place. Once the pitch of your roof is secure, add the panels and seal all of the joints to get a tight fit. Make sure there are no gaps between the joints before weatherproofing them. Finally, install gutters to make sure the roof doesn't leak to the ground below.

Installing windows is similar to installing roof panels. First, make sure you have a sturdy frame to insert the window into. If it's a double-pane window, you'll need to install it from inside of the greenhouse. If it's a single-pane window, you can install them from the outside. Either way, make sure you seal all of the joints to create a tight fit.

Installing doors is fairly simple because most greenhouses are designed with doors in mind. You can choose to have a custom door or have one made to fit your space. Make sure the door opens and closes smoothly, that it's properly sealed, and that it fits perfectly into its frame before adding weather stripping to the edges.

Step-By-Step Instructions

1. Placing Reinforcing Beams

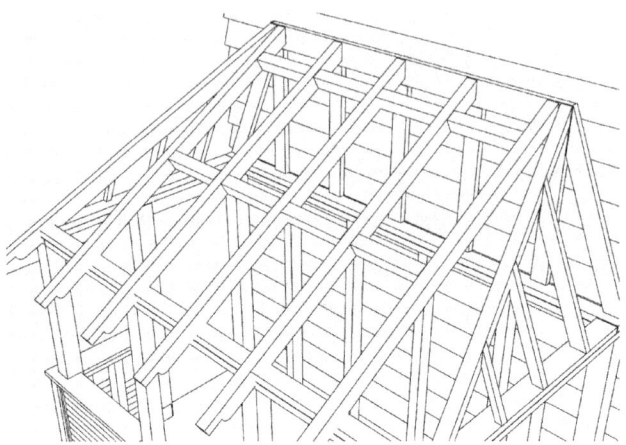

You can choose between a ridge beam and a polygon beam, but the result will be a sturdy roof that won't collapse on you. You'll have to get sturdy beams, long enough for the pitch of your roof, and the right width, so the panels fit around them. They should be about an inch and a half wider than your rafters, but smaller beams tend to make the roof look heavy. The best way to find out what beams you need is by checking the manufacturer's instructions.

2. Fastening the Roof Panels

You can fasten the roof panels with a rubber-gasket-equipped pole with barn screws driven every 12" at each rafter or purlin. Cut the side roof panels to fit and attach them with rubber gasket screws. This will ensure a tight seal and prevent water from seeping into the greenhouse. You can also use screws and/or nails to attach the side panels. This step is only necessary if you're using single-pane glass. The ridge and side panels should overlap each other to prevent rain from seeping into the greenhouse. There are three methods of applying the rubber gaskets on the side panels:

a. The first option is to attach the rubber gasket directly to the side panels. The rubber gasket should be at least twice the width of each panel so you can provide an adequate weatherproof seal.

b. Your second option is to attach the rubber gasket to a firm strip of wood attached to the side panels. This is preferable if you're using a wooden frame.

c. You can also attach the rubber gasket to a metal strip that's then attached to the inside of the wooden frame. This is preferable when you're using metal panels because they tend not to warp over time.

3. Attaching an Automatic Window Vent Opener

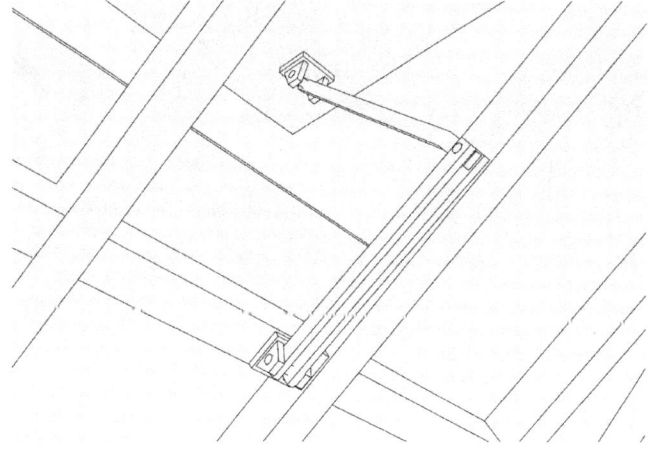

Attaching an automatic window vent opener is critical because it can help control the greenhouse's temperature. You can find vents with self-closing latches that open and close depending on the temperature. They're relatively inexpensive and easy to install. You can attach them directly to the frame of your greenhouse by screwing them in, adding a long wooden strip to serve as the counterweight, or using plastic ties attached to the vent itself and serve as the counterweight.

4. Covering the Gaps with Metal Flashing

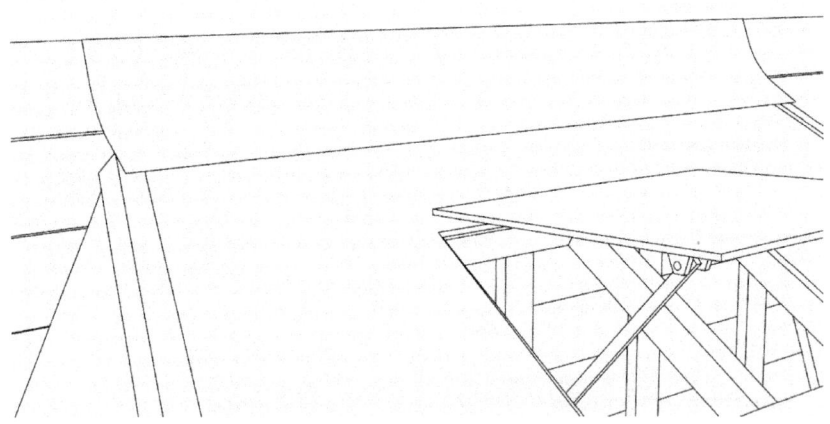

Cover any gaps between the roof panels with aluminum or galvanized metal flashing to protect the greenhouse from water seepage. Aluminum flashing of 12" width can be fastened to the house and lightly creased to extend over the gap and form a seal without any connection to the greenhouse. This flashing can be used instead of a rubber gasket. It's less expensive and easier to install. If you use metal, make sure it's rust-resistant. Overlap each piece of metal flashing by three inches so that water has no chance of seeping into the greenhouse.

5. Assembling the Window Frames

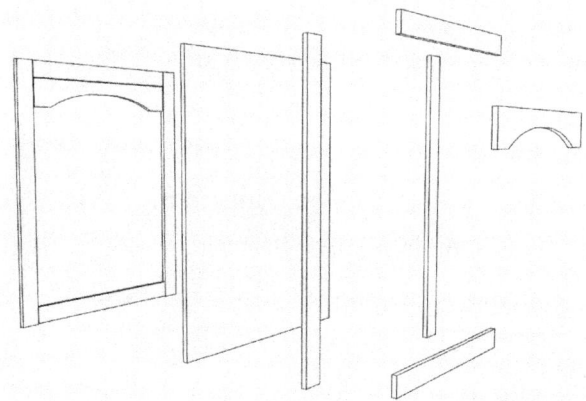

You can choose either to have custom-made windows or to replace your existing greenhouse windows with new ones. If you want to keep your original windows, you can attach plywood to the outside of them with nails or screws. If your greenhouse has standard-sized windows, you can find replacement ones that measure 23x36". If you're using vinyl or aluminum to construct your greenhouse, the window frame should be made of the same material. If you're using wood to construct your greenhouse, then the window frame should be made of plywood and treated so that it can resist water.

6. Attaching the Windows

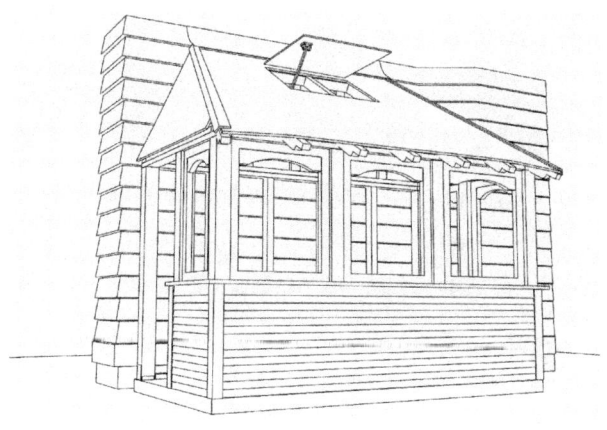

You can attach the standard-sized windows to your greenhouse's wooden frame by drilling a hole through the side panel and roof panel, then attaching the window to the top hole. You can also attach the windows with screws or nails, but make sure they're not too thin if your greenhouse is made of wood. You can also attach the window with a metal strip that's then attached to the wooden frame. This is best when your greenhouse is made of metal panels. Stop the molding on the perimeter of each window opening set so the window will be flush with the framed opening. It should overlap the window by at least one inch on all sides.

7. Assembling the Door Frame

You can choose to build a custom door or replace your existing greenhouse door. To replace the existing one, you'll need to remove it. Use nails or screws to attach the plywood door frame on the outside of your greenhouse's wooden frame, making sure it's not too close to the door opening but also that it's not too far away. Attach the rubber gasket to the door frame with staples or nails driven into the center of each side. You can then replace your existing door, making sure it fits snugly.

8. Hanging the Door

Once you have a custom door or a replacement greenhouse door, you can attach it to the rubber gasket with hinges. Make sure the hinge is not too tight or too loose. If it is, you may need to sand the metal. You can adjust the door's position and ensure it is level by using wedges. Attach one end of a wooden wedge to your greenhouse, then attach a smaller wooden wedge to the opposite end of that wedge. See where you can place these wedges so they're stable and won't slip. You can then attach the door hinges to these wedges, closing your greenhouse from the inside. It's best to paint first before you add the finishing touches.

Things to Remember Before and After Installing Your Windows and Doors

Don't forget to check if any part of the greenhouse needs repairs before installing your windows and doors. Check for cracks, holes, and corrosion. They will make it more difficult to install your roof, windows, or doors. You can use caulking if you need to fix any holes before you perform any installations.

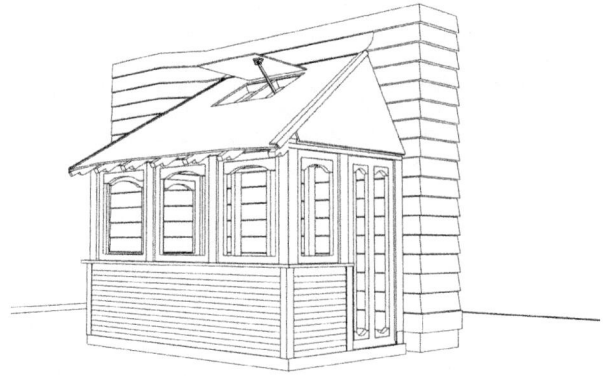

After installing your windows and doors, you should check to see that they fit snugly. If a caulking job has been done, check for cracks and holes. You can use a damp soapy cloth to do this. If you find any cracks or holes, you should patch them up immediately. You should also check your window and door locks to ensure they're working properly.

FAQs

- **What are the necessary tools for installing the roof, windows, and doors?**

  Tools you'll need include hammers, adjustable wrenches, screwdrivers, drill or electric saws, paintbrush, caulking gun, chisel, miter saw, wallboard saws.

- **How do you repair cracks in the greenhouse before installing the new roof, windows, or doors?**

  You can repair cracks with masonry paint. You can also fill any holes inside or outside your greenhouse with caulking.

- **What are the best types of windows to use in a greenhouse?**

  The best type of windows for a greenhouse include glass, polycarbonate, fiberglass, and acrylic.

- **What are some of the tools you need when installing doors in a greenhouse?**

  Tools needed for door installation include adjustable wrenches, a saw, a drill with screwdriver heads, and a caulking gun.

- **What should you do if the door or window is too tight?**

  You can use a rubber mallet to tap any loose areas gently. If that doesn't work, try sanding the metal. If your door lock isn't working properly, check if the bolts are too tight or too loose. If they are, you can remove the bolts and deal with them accordingly.

If you're interested in getting started with greenhouses, this guide should be your go-to resource. This chapter covered how to properly construct a greenhouse and install the roof, windows, and doors. We discussed what tools you might need and offered tips for making these installations. The materials and tools needed for installing these components include an adjustable wrench, drill, or electric saw. You should also know that materials include rubber gaskets, a wooden frame, glass windowpanes, and a wallboard saw.

Don't forget to check for cracks and holes before you install your windows or doors. You can fill any small holes with caulking and use masonry paint for larger holes. Also, make sure you check your locks before installing your windows or doors. The step-by-step instructions provided in this chapter should have been enough to help you install your greenhouse. Finally, this chapter ended with FAQs about installing the roof, windows, and doors. These questions should help you figure out how to troubleshoot problems you may encounter with your greenhouse.

Chapter 5: Greenhouse Irrigation Systems

This chapter explains everything you need to know about greenhouse irrigation systems. It starts by discussing the guidelines you should follow in choosing the best irrigation system and how to install it. The second part presents a few options of irrigation systems along with their pros and cons.

The Significance of a Greenhouse Irrigation System

A greenhouse irrigation system plays a critical role in watering your plants and preserving the nutrients by allowing water to drip gradually to the plant roots. A water supply pipe is installed above the soil or below the surface, depending on the type you choose. The primary objective of the irrigation system is to provide optimum nutrient and water levels directly to the plant roots to reduce evaporation and wastage.

The irrigation system consists of pipes, valves, tubing, and emitters that dispense water slowly. The system is efficient compared to other watering methods depending on how you operate and maintain it. You need to consult an expert before choosing the system that suits your greenhouse garden, soil, and types of plants.

The Benefits of Installing a Greenhouse Irrigation system

A greenhouse system uses filters to reduce issues like clogging. Water consists of small particles that can clog the emitters depending on the source. Filters help to trap these unwanted organisms to ensure the efficiency of the entire system.

Water Conservation

A greenhouse irrigation system conserves water by preventing deep drainage and evaporation. The water is directly supplied to the plant roots, so there is no wastage. This type of irrigation also plays a major role in eliminating many diseases that usually develop and spread when water comes into contact with foliage. The system provides high efficiency since water is delivered slowly and directly to the plant roots.

You can also use this irrigation method to provide soluble nutrients to the plants, and this will help increase crop yield. In arid places where water is often in short supply, the greenhouse irrigation system is the most preferred method. More importantly, the watering method is cost-effective and easy to install. You will save a lot of money in the long run if you choose this irrigation option.

Choosing a Quality Greenhouse Irrigation System

Choosing the appropriate irrigation system for your greenhouse garden seems easy, but the process can be daunting. Different factors should be considered before settling on a particular system that suits your needs. It is essential to enlist the services of an experienced company to assess your greenhouse garden and choose the best option available. You must deal with a licensed company with a good reputation in this particular area. You also need to check if the company offers a warranty in the event that the system develops problems within a specific time. Working with experts from the get-go will enhance your greenhouse's productivity.

How to Get the Best Greenhouse Irrigation System

It is crucial to select the best greenhouse watering system to ensure maximum growth of the plants. When selecting a watering system, you should get one that suits your needs and consider factors like the type of plants, size of greenhouse, and your budget. You also need to consider the pros and cons of each system. The following are some of the irrigation systems that you can consider.

Capillary Mats and Self-Watering Trays

This approach probably provides the easiest watering system for plants that do not require added water from above for smaller greenhouses. The self-watering trays provide water from below, and the mats release it slowly. The plants will never run out of moisture as long as the reservoirs have water. You need to fill them at least once every week, which makes them the easiest to maintain.

Pros

- Easy to install
- Saves energy and time
- Cost-effective
- Provides consistent supply of water
- Prevents risks of plant diseases

Cons

- Capillary mats can develop algae
- You need to fill the water manually
- The system might not suit all gardens

Over-head Sprinklers

This irrigation system is ideal for plants that require wet or misted foliage. It consists of pipes fitted with nozzles placed above the crops, and the spray ranges are adjusted. You can mount the sprinklers on the ceiling of the greenhouse garden. The sprinkler system is easy to operate, and it also saves time.

Pros

- Saves time

- Cost-effective

- Easy to automate and control

- Effective for coarse soil

Cons

- High operating costs

- Uses more water

- Promotes plant diseases as a result of excessive leaf wetness

- No customization of the system

Misting (Spray) System

The system is ideal for large greenhouses that have plenty of seeds that require regular watering. This watering method releases small quantities of water droplets in the form of mist. You can automate the misters to spray water for a specific period so they do not run continuously. Misters increase humidity in the greenhouse, and they are appropriate for the summer season or warmer climates.

Pros

- Cost-effective
- Ideal for tropical greenhouses
- Keeps the greenhouse cool
- Appropriate for a greenhouse that requires regular watering

Cons

- Wasteful and less efficient if managed poorly
- No water customization
- The humidity created is not suitable for all plants
- Overhead watering can cause plant diseases

Drip Irrigation Systems

The drip system is perfect since it is good for all purposes and also scalable to different sizes. The hose with multiple emitters provides a constant supply of water and soluble nutrients throughout the day to promote plant growth. The system reduces waste, and it can be automated to suit any size of greenhouse garden.

Pros

- The system can be programmed and automated
- Effective water distribution
- Reduces wastage of water
- Water can be reused
- Emitters are adjustable

Cons

- The method requires thorough cleaning and maintenance
- Requires power for the pump

- Can be costly to set up

- Clogging of the nozzles is possible

Soaker Hoses

This particular watering system resembles drip irrigation. The soaker hoses provide water from below. It does not have emitters making it perfect for people who do not want nozzles. The challenge with this watering method is that you cannot adjust the amount of water to certain areas, and it is not suitable for individual plants.

Pros

- Easy to install and low maintenance

- Inexpensive

- Promotes water conservation

- No worries about clogging

- Can be automated

Cons

- Water distribution cannot be adjusted

- The water pipes must be level

- Repairs and maintenance can be challenging

Off-Grid Solar-Powered Greenhouse Irrigation Systems

This solar-powered irrigation system can provide water in the form of drips, and it's suitable for smaller greenhouse gardens. This is probably the most cost-effective system since it uses power from the sun.

Pros

- No electricity and fuel costs

- Less maintenance and labor

- Environmentally friendly (no greenhouse gasses emitted)

Cons

- Only works during the day
- High initial costs
- Lower productivity in cold seasons

Reasons for Choosing Automated vs. Manual Irrigation Systems

If you are looking for a stress-free irrigation system, you can consider an automated one. This type works on a timer and provides your crops with the same amount of water. If you have a bigger greenhouse garden, you may need to consider this watering system instead of a manual one. The following are the advantages and disadvantages of automated irrigation systems.

Saves Time

The major reason why you must pick an automated irrigation system is that it saves time. If you have a bigger greenhouse garden, it can be time-consuming to water it manually.

Improves Efficiency

Automatic watering systems improve efficiency and also eliminate issues like overwatering or under-watering.

Focus on Other Tasks

An automatic watering system gives you time to perform other tasks like weeding, trimming, feeding, or pollinating your plants. In other words, you get ample time to do other activities in your garden.

Cost-Effective

An automated watering system helps ensure that water is distributed effectively to the plants without wastages, helping you cut costs in water bills.

Disadvantages of Automated Watering Systems

Automated irrigation systems are relatively expensive to install, especially if you have a big garden. The installation process is time-consuming, depending on the system you choose. However, other systems are easy to install. If the system is not properly installed, you will likely experience faults that lead to water wastage.

Which Is the Best Greenhouse Irrigation System?

Now that you know the pros and cons of the most common greenhouse irrigation systems, your ultimate choice is a matter of personal preference. You can automate all irrigation systems if you want. However, the drip irrigation system is the best since it provides a constant water supply from the ground to the plants. It also conserves water better than other watering methods like overhead sprinklers. To pick the best irrigation system, you must consider your needs.

Installing a Greenhouse Irrigation System

The overhead sprinkler system is easy to install, and you can do it yourself as long as you have the right tools and supplies required. The following are the supplies you will need for an overhead greenhouse irrigation system:

- Drip irrigation hose
- Pipe connectors
- Shrub sprinkler heads
- Pipe tee connectors
- Sprinkler head risers
- Garden hose connector
- Garden watering timer
- Pipe thread tape
- Poly tubing
- Garden hose splitter
- Tape measure
- PVC pipe saw
- Zip ties

Installation Steps for an Overhead Greenhouse Sprinkler System

The following are the simple steps you should follow when installing your overhead sprinkler system.

Step 1: The first step is to consider the number of sprinkler heads you need for your greenhouse garden. You should space the sprinklers at least 6 to 7 feet high to ensure plenty of overlap.

Step 2: Use poly end tubing to cap one of the ends of the mainline to block water before you install the sprinkler heads.

Step 3: Install the sprinkler heads on the tubing. Use a PVC cutting saw to ensure that the heads are properly fixed. You must measure the distance between the sprinkler heads along with the poly tubing.

Step 4: When you have installed the sprinkler heads, the next step is to place the hose fitting to the end of the tubing. Once done, you are ready to place the final faucet hose fitting. Take correct measurements of the overhead sprinkler tubing system and attach it at the end.

Step 5: When you have assembled everything, test the system, and check for issues like leaks before installing the system onto the greenhouse ceiling. Use a pipe thread to fix all the leaks that you find along the pipes.

Step 6: The final step is to install the overhead sprinkler system for your greenhouse garden. Ensure the pipes are fixed in the right place, and no loose connections can disturb the smooth flow of water.

When you have installed your overhead sprinkler system, you can automate it using a garden watering timer. You simply plug your garden hose into the timer then set it. However, you should check your greenhouse garden regularly to ensure that it is getting sufficient water. The advantage of automating your greenhouse watering system is that it makes your life easier.

Manual irrigation can be physically demanding and is also time-consuming. However, automation helps you perform other tasks while the system supplies water to your crops. The DIY sprinkler option is lightweight and easy to install. All you need to do is constantly inspect the irrigation system for potential faults.

The success of a greenhouse garden depends on the quality of the irrigation system you use. As discussed above, it is essential to choose an irrigation system that is easy to install and use. You have also learned about the advantages and disadvantages of different irrigation systems you can consider for your garden.

Chapter 6: Temperature and Humidity

A greenhouse garden requires a controlled temperature that is ideal for specific types of crops. There should also be proper humidity inside your greenhouse, and you can achieve this by using proper tools to monitor humidity and temperature. This chapter discusses the measures you can take to control both temperature and humidity. People who live in temperate climates, tropical regions, or arid regions require varying temperature and humidity ranges for their greenhouse gardens. The chapter covers recommended temperatures and humidity for fruit, vegetables, flowers, and herbs in different regions.

Temperature Considerations for Greenhouse Gardens

If you love to plant different crops in your greenhouse garden, you should know the optimal temperatures required to get the best yield. It is generally recommended that the optimal temperature for a greenhouse garden should be 27°C since anything higher than that can damage your plants. However, you must know that the types of plants you have inside your greenhouse determine the ideal temperature that should be maintained. Temperature supports the growth of your plants and affects the yield you are likely to get.

Crops like tomatoes and melons require warmer temperatures to increase productivity. You can observe the leaves of your plants to see if you have an optimal temperature. Plants with brown leaves or bruised skin show that they are exposed to insufficient or excessive temperatures. As you will see below, there are temperature ranges expected for different types of crops in greenhouse gardens.

The Appropriate Temperature for a Greenhouse

It is generally accepted that the ideal temperature for a greenhouse garden is 27°C or 81°F. This temperature is sufficient enough to keep your plants healthy. If the temperature exceeds 27°C, it can kill your plants. For instance, tomatoes are likely to grow poorly when the temperature exceeds 32°C (90°F) during the day and drops to 24°C (75°F) at night.

Most plants, including vegetables, herbs, flowers, and fruit, do well at 27°C. Since the plants will be growing under artificial conditions, it is vital to maintain constant control of the greenhouse's temperature. Failure to control the temperature inside the greenhouse can impact crops. The following are some of the measures you should consider controlling the temperature inside the greenhouse.

Controlling Temperature inside the Greenhouse

Many diseases thrive in conditions that are characterized by high temperatures and humidity. Warmer temperatures can lead to increased humidity levels in the air, affecting your plants' quality. On the other hand, a lower temperature can impact plant growth. Therefore, it is important to control humidity and temperature in the greenhouse.

A greenhouse is specifically designed to trap heat from the sun. The amount of sunshine and ventilation in the greenhouse controls both temperature and humidity. The excessive temperature inside is not good for the plants. You can control the temperature by opening the vents in the greenhouse. In some instances, an air conditioning system is ideal for regulating temperature. You can also install a heater that you can use during the winter when the temperatures are usually low.

You must also choose the appropriate time to grow your plants. The winter season is generally cooler, so you may need to generate warmth via artificial means. The challenge with using artificial warmers is that it consumes more power. When you think there is too much humidity inside the greenhouse, draw in some fresh air from outside. You can also use artificial lights to imitate the sun. Greenhouse heaters also play a crucial role in providing the much-needed temperature by the plants. These artificial heating and cooling methods are designed to convince the crops that they are going through a specific season.

Tools Required for Greenhouse Temperature Monitoring

There is a specific tool that you will need to track humidity and temperature inside your greenhouse. A wireless greenhouse monitoring system for temperature is one important tool you can consider. This option is convenient since it allows you to monitor temperature and humidity fluctuations online. This technology allows you to get real-time data about the temperature and humidity inside your greenhouse.

A greenhouse offers an artificial environment, so it must be properly maintained to ensure there are no steep variations in the temperature and humidity – especially true if you are growing off-season plants. Apart from maintaining your greenhouse, you need to install a temperature alarm in your greenhouse. This instrument helps identify problems like temperature fluctuations, power outages, water damages, or intrusion of undesirable elements. This monitoring system provides dependable results about the cooling and heating options inside your greenhouse.

Despite the outdoor weather, you can still control the temperature inside your greenhouse, helping you maintain the temperature at an optimum level. Temperature sensors are also ideal for your greenhouse, and they provide you with accurate and real-time data. With an appropriate temperature gauge, you can easily check the lowest and highest temperatures over 24 hours.

You need to check the temperature in the evening and early morning to understand the temperature changes. This will also help you understand how these changes affect the growth of your plants. As you are going to see below, greenhouse temperatures are affected by different seasons.

Summer Temperature for Greenhouse

During the summer season, greenhouses can get extra hot, which is why temperatures must be controlled. Many crops cannot thrive in conditions characterized by extremely high temperatures. As you have observed above, the perfect temperature for summer is 27°C or 81°F. There are also optimal humidity and temperatures for greenhouse growing that you should know.

The optimal temperature and humidity set points for cultivation are as follows.

Temperature Range	18°-24°C (64°F – 75°F)
Relative Humidity	80%

The optimal relative humidity for a greenhouse is 80% for most plants. Humidity is a critical component you should consider when you want to cultivate any crop. At 80%, the growth rate of a plant is at its highest. However, humidity levels that are higher or lower than the optimal rate can lead to lower quality output or slower growth of the plants. The challenge with high humidity is that it can increase common diseases and problems like powdery mildew and botrytis. Humidity is a vital parameter that each grower should understand. Try to maintain relative humidity at the desired level for optimum productivity.

Another important element you should know concerns the ideal temperature for cultivation. You will need temperature ranges of about 18°-24oC (64°F – 75°F) for most greenhouse crops. Any temperature that is outside this range can impact the growth of the plants and crop quality. It is essential to control humidity and temperature for different greenhouse crops. Crops that are not getting optimal humidity or temperature are characterized by slower growth and poor quality.

Uncontrolled humidity will lead to condensation inside the structure, which further leads to diseases.

Reducing Humidity in the Air

To control humidity and temperature in the greenhouse, you need to consider different things like shade and ventilation, as explained in detail below. The fall and spring times are usually characterized by an increase in humidity-related diseases in greenhouses. Sunny conditions and warmer temperatures increase evaporation from the soil and transpiration from the leaves. Warm air holds moisture, and when the temperatures drop at night, condensation will form on the leaves and other surfaces. As a result, water droplets will form, and this will promote the development of pathogen spores.

Dripping water will promote the spread of pathogens to other plants. You should know that there is a strong correlation between temperature and humidity. High humidity is closely associated with warm temperatures. When managing humidity inside your greenhouse, you should know that this relationship is very important. You should know that high humidity, especially in an enclosed area, forms a breeding ground for pathogens and bacteria that can affect the health of your crops.

Reducing Humidity

You should ensure adequate plant spacing and appropriate watering to maintain the desired level of humidity. You should also make sure that the floor is well-drained and there is free circulation of fresh air inside the greenhouse. You must keep the greenhouse dry, especially at night when the temperatures are likely to drop. Water on the surfaces can evaporate, adding moisture to the air, which makes the environment humid. High humidity will remove the energy that is meant to keep the house warm.

You should provide sufficient water to the plants to prevent wetting the floors and other surfaces inside the greenhouse. It is essential to water your plants in the morning to allow excess water to dry during the day before evening. The highest humidity is usually found around the plant canopy. Therefore, it is imperative to space your plants out to promote free air circulation, preventing any humidity buildup. Weeds inside the greenhouse can also contribute to high humidity. It is essential to keep your greenhouse free from grass and other unwanted covering plants.

You can also supply bottom heat to improve air circulation inside the plant foliage to prevent condensation on the surfaces. The heat can go a long way in keeping the plants warm, which helps to reduce condensation. You should make sure that condensation is reduced inside your greenhouse.

Ventilation and Heating

Ventilation and heating are crucial in reducing humidity inside your greenhouse. Ventilation will allow the exchange of moist air in the greenhouse with drier air from outside. Since outdoor air is dry, it has an increased ability to hold moisture, thereby reducing condensation. Venting helps moderate the amount of moisture in the air to prevent condensation inside the house. With this in mind, you must install an appropriate heating and ventilation system in your greenhouse. With proper ventilation, warm air that holds moisture is eliminated from the house. You must do the heating and venting at least two or three times an hour in the evening.

Desirable Humidity Level

You need to buy a device that can measure humidity to heat and vent your greenhouse efficiently. The temperature determines the desirable humidity inside your greenhouse. If you are in warmer environments, the plants can tolerate high humidity. When you are in cooler temperatures, the plants will need lower relative humidity. The table below shows the corresponding relative humidity and temperature set points that are ideal for disease prevention.

Temperature (°F)	Humidity
50°F	83%
61°F	89%
68°F	91%
86°F	95%

Air Movement

It is vital to control air movement in the greenhouse if you want to manage diseases effectively. Continual air movement is essential since it helps to maintain a balance of temperature inside the facility. Air movement also helps ensure that the greenhouse's interior is cool and the plants are not badly impacted. If artificial ventilation does not sufficiently cool the air, you can run fans or an air conditioner. Other heating and cooling systems for greenhouses have sensors, and they automatically turn on to maintain a balance in temperature and humidity. If there is too much humidity in the air, you must cool it. Make sure all exhausts are working properly.

To promote the healthy growth of your crops and achieve high productivity, you should maintain optimum greenhouse temperatures suitable for different plants. Generally, the optimal temperature for a greenhouse garden should be around 27°C during the day and about 24°C (75°F) at night. As you have observed above, greenhouse temperatures mainly depend on the type of crop you have. With the right tools, it is so easy to monitor and control the temperature of your greenhouse. You must constantly check the greenhouse's intelligent humidity and temperature control system. A temperature control vent is ideal for controlling the humidity inside the greenhouse. You can also observe the plants to check if they are getting sufficient humidity and temperature.

Chapter 7: Ventilation and Lighting

This chapter discusses the importance of ventilation and lighting in your greenhouse garden. The first section focuses on two types of ventilation that include natural and mechanical ventilation systems. It outlines different types of ventilation ideal for various types of plants like fruit, vegetables, flowers, and herbs. The second part explains the different types of lighting appropriate for different types of greenhouses.

https://unsplash.com/photos/yellow-and-purple-flowers-in-greenhouse-mG3abK1CBOY

The Significance of a Greenhouse Ventilation System

One of the main reasons for growing plants in a greenhouse is eliminating factors like pests and unreliable weather conditions. However, growers need to consider ventilation for their greenhouse. Ventilation is a process that involves the exchange of indoor air with outside air. Ventilation plays a pivotal role in a greenhouse since it promotes cooling, heat removal, enhances air circulation, and provides fresh carbon dioxide (CO_2) for crops.

Regular exchange of air in a greenhouse is vital since it allows plants to thrive while at the same time promoting a healthy temperature range. When there is too much moisture in the air, it can lead to plant diseases. Extremely high or low temperatures can affect the growth of your plants. You need an active cooling system that maintains a balance in temperature and humidity to ensure optimal growth of the crops.

Choosing the Appropriate Greenhouse Ventilation System

There are different methods and tools you can consider getting proper ventilation. You can either use passive or active ventilation methods depending on the type of greenhouse and the geographical area where it is located. Natural ventilation (NV) includes the use of vents on the structure, while mechanical ventilation (MV) consists of high-volume fans. Alternatively, you can consider a combination of both NV and MV for effective results.

Natural Ventilation (NV)

As the name suggests, NV mainly relies on natural forces to promote the exchange of indoor and outdoor air, and it is the most energy-efficient option you can consider for your greenhouse. The direction of the wind and the quantity of air can be unpredictable when you use NV for greenhouse ventilation. It is essential to utilize openings on the structure to allow wind inside that will create positive pressure. This pressure then pushes the inside air outside to create a moderate environment.

You should choose the right position for your greenhouse, like putting the vents' openings in the appropriate direction. This strategy helps you take advantage of the wind direction to enhance the quality ventilation of your greenhouse without using any source of power, which can be costly.

Natural ventilation (NV) is significantly improved when your greenhouse has several vent locations that allow the air to enter from one side then exit from the opposite side. This means that you must have strategic ventilation points to allow the free movement of air in all directions. You should have strategic ventilation points in the greenhouse to take advantage of passive ventilation. You can include different forms of ventilation, like wall vents, roll-up sides, and roof vents. The roof vents are designed to let hot and stale air out, while roll-up sides and wall vents allow air to get inside the greenhouse. If you choose this option, you should know that you cannot control passive ventilation. You can enjoy the full benefits of this ventilation method when the situation is available.

You can also concentrate on thermal buoyancy to ventilate your structure. Thermal buoyancy is when hot air rises to allow fresh and cool air to enter the structure and push the hot air outward. This buoyancy is achieved when solar radiation generates hot air above the plant canopy inside the structure. The hot air inside will escape through the roof openings. The air will be trapped inside if there are no vents on the roof. NV via thermal buoyancy mainly applies to greenhouses with plants that can actively transpire and cool through evaporation.

The buoyancy ventilation method is also prevalent when the air outside is hotter than the air inside. Hot air specifically likes to move from areas characterized by higher temperatures to places with lower temperatures. This method is effective in cool weather where the outside temperature is cooler than inside. As a result, this leads to a cooling effect inside the structure. However, there are certain days when there will not be enough air which can impact the quality of your crops. You cannot solely rely on passive ventilation for commercial gardening.

Mechanical Ventilation (MV)

Mechanical ventilation consists of fans to facilitate the exchange of internal air with the air coming from outside. The size of the fans is determined by establishing the cooling requirements of your greenhouse. This involves the replenishment of CO_2 and the removal of moisture. The main difference between MV and NV is that MV provides predictable and sufficient air exchange. It also offers a consistent direction of airflow, and you can also control it to suit the needs of your plants.

The fans can use positive displacement to push air into the greenhouse or use negative displacement to pull the air out of the greenhouse. To achieve positive displacement, one fan at the end of the greenhouse will push the air from outside through an overhead plastic duct positioned on the center of the greenhouse roof. This duct consists of holes that will blow air over the plants.

This type of mechanical ventilation was popular in the northern climates around the '60s and '70s, where a furnace connected to the duct would heat the air coming from outside. However, the overhead duct can cast shadows over the plants, which can make the method unpopular. Additionally, the heated air is poorly distributed, and it also results in high energy costs.

Nowadays, the MV ducts are placed below the benches, and there are relief vents on the other side of the greenhouse to prevent a situation of over-pressurization. If this happens, the structure can bow outward, and doors swing open. The doors may remain shut, which will affect your capability to control the environment.

Negative displacement is the traditional method of mechanical ventilation often used in greenhouses. Large-volume axial fans located on the walls of the interior of the greenhouse are used. The fans pull air from outside through the opposite vents. The exhaust vents provide many benefits, such as controlling the amount of air exchanged – depending on your plants' needs. The method uses low energy compared to the use of positive displacement fans or air conditioning.

Another aspect is that the fan speed can be controlled to suit your desired needs. Unlike natural ventilation, the main advantage of this particular method is that it is possible to control the volume of air that is exchanged. You can also save energy by limiting the speed of the fans, and this will also ensure that the motors will last longer as a result of reduced load.

As you have observed in the previous sections, the biggest advantage of growing plants in a greenhouse is that you can use climate management technology. Whatever the climate you have in your environment, you can enjoy optimum yield if you choose the right ventilation strategy for your greenhouse gardening. To be on the safe side, it is essential to utilize both natural and mechanical ventilation methods.

Choosing Lighting for Your Greenhouse

There are different things you should consider when choosing to light for your greenhouse. You must choose the appropriate spectrum that all plants need - Photosynthetically Active Radiation (PAR) light. This kind of radiation consists of a wavelength range of about 400 to 700 nm. Supplemental light is vital for the growth of your crops and the yield you are likely to get.

When looking for appropriate lighting for your greenhouse, you must consider the available sunlight, the type of plants, and the time of the year you are growing them. Your greenhouse requires about 6 hours of direct light every day. If there is no sufficient sunlight, you need to consider supplemental lighting, which involves high-intensity artificial lights designed to promote plant growth and yield. There are a few lighting options you can consider for your greenhouse garden, and some of them are outlined below.

High-Pressure Sodium (Hps) Fixtures

HPS provides intense and bright light, and it also has a long lifespan. This fixture has a proven track record for many growers, and it remains popular since it works well for all plants. The fixture is energy efficient, and it is a cheaper option compared to other types of lighting available on the market. You should mount the high-pressure sodium lights about 30 to 60 inches above the crops for optimal results.

Ceramic Metal Halide

Ceramic metal halide lamps provide blue light, although they appear bright white to the naked eye. These fixtures can function as primary sources of light, and they have a lifespan of about 8,000 to 15,000 hours. These lights are more efficient than other types of incandescent bulbs, and they are a perfect option for places that do not get sufficient natural light. The fixtures must warm for five minutes before they provide full light. The halide lamps are not recommended for areas characterized by an unreliable power supply. The lamps should be positioned about 30 to 36 inches above the plants. These lights are often used when the plants are in their early growth stage – and they are dimmable.

T5 Fixtures

TX fixtures are the most popular and efficient fluorescent lighting for the greenhouse. They consume less energy and have a lifespan of up to 50 000 hours. The fixtures are environmentally friendly and can be used during the initial growth stage up to full growth. The fixture produces limited heat, so it is ideal to place it very close to the plant – about 6 to 12 inches.

LED Lighting

Light-emitting diode (LED) lighting is energy efficient compared to other crop lights. However, the setup costs of LED lighting and its success in greenhouses can be concerning for most growers. This type of lighting can reduce energy costs by about 75%, and it comes with lower maintenance. The lights are available in different temperatures and colors and are also adjustable. For greater efficiency, you can place the fixture closer to the plants.

What to Consider when Choosing Lighting

There are different things you should consider getting the perfect lighting system for your greenhouse. The following are some of the critical elements that can help you make an informed decision.

https://unsplash.com/photos/turned-on-fluorescent-light-PHWNavVdvbc

Know the Light Level Requirements

It is critical to check the light level requirements for your greenhouse garden. Supplemental lighting should be a fraction of the complete natural light levels. Therefore, you must measure the light level and supplemental light requirements first. Additionally, you must check the light fixture that is likely to cast a shadow which can block natural light.

The Efficiency of the Light Fixture

You should also check the efficiency of the light fixture before purchasing it. Energy costs can impact your greenhouse business, so you need to weigh the potential expenses after the initial investment. Consider all the requirements to power your greenhouse to ensure that you get an ideal system.

Quality ventilation and lighting are essential to the success of your greenhouse garden. Ventilation promotes the free circulation of air to create a balance between temperature and humidity, which are good for plant growth. Ventilation also helps prevent plant diseases that can be caused by excess moisture or humidity in the environment. It is essential to choose the ideal ventilation method that suits your greenhouse. On top of that, you also need to get the right lighting for your plants since they require light to promote photosynthesis. You must consult an expert to determine the ideal type of lighting for your greenhouse.

Chapter 8: Growing Vegetables

This chapter covers how to grow vegetables in the greenhouse. When building your own greenhouse, it's important to make sure you have a plan for what you want to grow. In this chapter, we'll give you tips on making a diagram of your crops and choosing which vegetables are best for growing indoors, and a lot more. Once that's done, it should be easy from there!

https://unsplash.com/photos/orange-pumpkin-Pv_Mut-lvWg

Planning for Your Vegetable Greenhouse

Planning is a valuable part of any project. It can be easy to get excited about building a greenhouse and just start putting things together without any sort of plan in place, but this is not recommended. To begin designing your plan for the greenhouse, it's important to have a general idea of what you want your finished product to look like. We recommend using graph paper for this because it will help to get all of the measurements right. Once you've got an outline sketched out, start adding specific details such as where windows are and what type of shelves or growing beds you will need.

Mapping Out Your Vegetable Garden

Now that you know how much space each vegetable will need, it's time to plan where everything will go! Use your diagram and sketch the layout of the greenhouse on a piece of graph paper. Ensure there's enough space for things like pathways between groups of plants so they don't get too crowded/overgrown – while still making sure there's enough space for all the plants themselves.

Don't forget to leave room for aisles! It can be easy to not think about these things when planning out your garden, but they're important so that you don't have too many large pathways between groups of vegetables and end up with overcrowding or bare soil patches. You need to be able to have easy access to your plants.

This is your chance to be creative! If you're not happy with the way things look, it's easy enough to move some plants around or switch up where they go. Have fun with it, and don't feel like you have too many restrictions on how everything should look. These vegetables aren't going anywhere anytime soon so take advantage of being able to get creative!

Refer to the instructions on the seed package to determine how far apart your seeds should be from each other. For example, if a plant needs at least eight inches of space to grow well, it will say so on the instructions. It's also important to remember that some vegetables need more room than others *from the seedling stage* until they're fully grown and producing fruit/vegetables. This is especially true of larger plants like tomatoes and carrots.

The Best Vegetables to Grow in a Greenhouse

Ideally, the vegetables you want to grow should be able to thrive in a greenhouse environment. This means they need lots of sunlight but not too much heat and will benefit from having warm soil as long as it's moist enough for their roots to survive.

Tomatoes are probably one of the best choices because they do well with plenty of sun! They also grow quickly, so they won't take up much space for long. They are also great to have in your greenhouse because you can pick them at different stages of growth depending on when you want to eat/use them, whether it's cherry tomatoes right off the vine or ripe, juicy ones that are ready to be used in cooking!

https://unsplash.com/photos/tomatoes-hanging-on-tomato-plant-lLiUI-Y2mI8

Peppers need a lot of sun but aren't particularly picky about the temperature. They also tend to grow quickly, so they won't be in your greenhouse for too long, which is nice because you can enjoy them months after starting them indoors!

Carrots are great if your soil isn't very rich or moist. Their roots need dry, compacted earth to grow healthy and strong. They tend to take a while for their roots to develop, so they may not produce anything in the first few months, but it's worth waiting!

Broccoli is one of those plants that do well with lots of sunlight. They grow quickly and don't need too much water during their growing period, but they require fairly rich soil to produce large heads! If you're concerned about having enough space inside your greenhouse because there are already too many tall vegetables, broccoli may not be the best option.

Cauliflower is another plant that gets tall fast, so it might not work well in small spaces. It also takes longer than some vegetables to start producing cauliflower florets, so you may want to wait until the summer if that's an issue.

Beets are a great choice because they grow quickly and can handle being inside! They don't require much sunlight or water, so they're also very easy but still produce a lot of food! Their roots need soil with good drainage. However, wet soil isn't ideal for their growth process.

Pumpkins aren't great for small spaces because they grow very tall. You'll probably need to cover them with a shade cloth if it's too warm in your greenhouse, or else you risk the pumpkin fruits overproducing! They also require lots of room underground so that their roots can develop properly.

French beans are an easy choice for anyone who doesn't have much growing space to work with! They grow quickly and produce a lot of beans, so it's worth starting with enough plants in case you decide you want them as often as possible.

Lettuce is another great option because they don't require too many resources - just water, some compost or fertilizer if you have it, and decent drainage. They don't need much sun, so they grow well inside the greenhouse – even with tall plants nearby!

Potatoes are also a great choice because they don't require many resources. They need warmer soil than most other vegetables, though. If it's cold in your greenhouse, you may want to start them indoors and only plant outside when the weather starts warming up!

Herbs are some of the best choices for any gardener because they are so simple to grow. You can even start them indoors if your greenhouse is too cold! Basil, cilantro, parsley, and thyme do well in small spaces. They don't need much water or sunlight, but they do require good drainage.

What to Plant, and Where

The greenhouse has to be planned to keep in mind what you want to grow, the space available, and what kind of climate it is.

Short Fruit Bearing Plants

Shorter plants that bear fruit should be towards the south. Many of the veggies and herbs can only be grown on the South edge. This is where they get the steadiest sunshine exposure without being blocked by any of the garden Goliaths. Peppers, eggplants, strawberries, spinach, and arugula thrive in brighter areas.

Plants that Need Shade

The north side is a good choice for plants that need shade. These include leafy vegetables that grow upward but don't bear fruit, such as lettuce and cabbage leaves. These plants also do well in the middle of the garden.

Vines that Don't Need a Trellis

The west side is a good choice for plants that need to be contained, such as peas and beans. These also do well near the middle or at the southern edge of your garden, with taller companions like cucumber vines. These plants grow very fast and might overshadow the smaller plants if grown in the middle of the garden bed.

Root Vegetables

Root vegetables can be grown anywhere in the garden, typically near the center. They do not require much space and will grow fine even if they are crowded together. The plants that work well as root crops include carrots, potatoes, radish, and turnips.

Growing Taller Plants

The taller plants such as tomatoes, peppers, and eggplants can be trained to grow vertically by using a trellis. The north side is the best choice for growing these tall vegetables as they will not shade shorter plants below them.

Efficient Layout Options

You have more choices when it comes to growing in pots, tubs, or bags. You may relocate the plants as needed, and the soil will be somewhat warmer. Purpose-built staging/shelving for potted plants and seeds ensures that your plants get the light and warmth they need while increasing your growing area. Any shelving you install should have adequate drainage and allow light to reach the plants beneath it.

Hanging brackets may be used to help create vertical string lines for tomato or bean plant cultivation, for example. Bees can be enticed to help pollinate the plants inside the greenhouse by placing a hanging flower basket at the entrance.

Raised Beds

Raised beds are a great choice for indoor gardening because they don't require as much soil and take up less space. You may also modify the edge of your greenhouse to accommodate raised beds, allowing you to have more options when it comes to what goes where.

How to Select Pots for Your Greenhouse Vegetables

You may either grow vegetables in pots or on the ground, and they both have their advantages and disadvantages. On the one hand, you may move planters around to suit your needs, while on the other hand, growing in-ground vegetables is easier for some people because there's less work involved with digging a big hole!

In addition to having more control over where your plants are located, potted veggies will fare better if you don't have to deal with the weight of heavy soil. Another advantage is that containers can be placed up against brick or stone walls inside your greenhouse without worrying about it getting wet, so they are ideal for areas where drainage may not be great.

The biggest disadvantage of growing vegetables in containers is that you'll need to fill them with good potting mix every year because the soil will only last for one season before becoming depleted. You can also use old compost or other organic matter to fill your pots, which you could alternatively put into raised beds in-ground if you're not growing veggies! There are also seedling trays that help sprout your plants indoors with less mess and fuss, which is ideal if you're new to gardening or prefer starting off small!

Pot Types

You may use pots, tubs, and bags/containers for growing your vegetables. Pots are ideal if you want to move them around or place them up against brick walls without worrying about the soil getting wet.

Tub-type containers such as strawberry planters allow you to grow larger plants with deeper roots, which is helpful if you want to grow things like cucumbers and beans. Bags, such as potato bags or compost bags, are especially useful if your greenhouse is small because these containers require less space than pots.

Pot Sizes

For shorter plants that don't shade out sun-sensitive crops below them (such as lettuce), it's ideal for the container to be around 12 to 18 inches high. For taller plants, such as cucumbers and tomatoes, you'll need a container that's at least 24 inches deep, so the plant has space for its roots.

When it comes to planting seeds, ensure that any containers are wide enough at the top, so there's room for the seeds to grow.

You can also use bigger pots than the plant's root ball, which will allow for more growth and give your plants room to spread their roots as they grow larger.

Soil Considerations

When choosing your soil, remember that drainage is key, so you should never plant veggies in a regular potting mix. This type of soil tends to get waterlogged and drown your plants or create a breeding ground for mold and other fungi.

Soil type selection also depends on your vegetable variety, as some plants grow better in different kinds of soil. For example, vegetables such as broccoli and cabbage require a rich loam to produce good heads, while carrots do well in sandy soils that allow for deeper root growth.

In general, you'll want to use potting mix or compost-enriched potting soil if you're growing in pots because this will last longer when you're using containers. If you opt to grow your vegetables in the ground, ensure that the soil is well-draining and contains plenty of organic matter or compost!

Consider the following soil mixes:

Potting Mix - A mixture of loam, peat moss, and vermiculite

Peat Moss - Can be replaced by coir or coconut fibers as coir is made from the husks of coconuts which are usually considered waste material in most parts of Asia. So, it is environmentally friendly too!

Compost-Enriched Potting Soil - A mixture of compost and regular potting mix that may or may not contain peat moss

Raised Bed Soil - If you have access to rich, well-draining raised bed soil from your yard, this is the ideal choice as it will provide plants with nutrients for longer!

Planting Vegetables: The Step-by-Step Guide

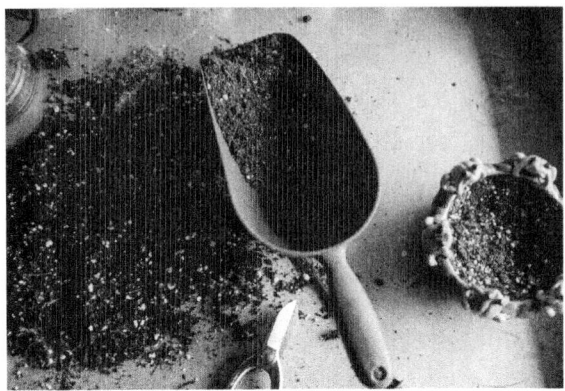

Preparing the Soil

It's important to prepare the soil before you plant your vegetables. Start by adding a mixture of compost and potting mix or other organic matter (such as lawn clippings) into your container if using pots.

Ensure that any new plants are well-watered before planting so it isn't too dry in the beginning stages because this may cause the plant to wilt or die.

Planting Your Seeds or Seedlings

When planting seeds, try spacing them about an inch apart if they're tiny seedlings such as carrots and radishes because these vegetables require less room for growth. If you're growing larger veggie varieties like tomatoes, space your seeds at least two inches apart because these vegetables need more room for root growth.

Once you've planted your seeds, water the soil until it's soaked but not muddy because this may wash away any seedlings that are just starting to grow, it can take anywhere from one week to three weeks after planting before new leaves start emerging, so be patient! If you notice anything unusual like mold, mildew, or spots on the leaves during this time period, you should contact your local extension service to find out what's causing it.

Transplanting Seedlings

If you've planted seeds in your containers and the seedling hasn't grown well, or at all, there's a chance that it may not be getting enough nutrients. This is usually due to overcrowding, so you should transplant them into bigger pots if this is the case. Make sure that any new container has proper drainage and can hold the weight of the soil and plant.

Pruning Your Vegetables

After you've planted your vegetables, it's important to keep them healthy and happy. This means pruning the plants every few weeks, depending on their growth rate or how large they are. For smaller seedlings like lettuce, make sure that any yellowed leaves are removed because these aren't getting enough sun exposure to produce healthy greens.

If you're growing larger vegetables like zucchini or cucumbers, remove any flowers that appear because these plants focus on producing fruit instead of leaves once they've flowered. This also helps prevent insects from laying eggs in the blooms and spreading disease to your vegetables!

Watering Your Vegetables

It's important to water your plants regularly because this will help them grow well and produce delicious fruit or veggies! Make sure that the soil is moist but not muddy at all times. If you're growing in containers, check if they need more water by poking a finger into the top layer of dirt.

Watering Methods

Hand-Watering - Usually done with a watering can and is the most common method.

Watering Hose - If you have access to one of these, this will make it easy to reach all areas of your garden.

Sprinkler or Soaker Hose - Only used on younger plants as they may get waterlogged with heavier watering methods such as hand-watering.

Water Quality

It's important to use the right kind of water for your plants because it can have a huge impact on their growth and their state of health. Ensure that you don't use softened or distilled water when watering your vegetables because this may cause them to wilt, dry out, or become discolored!

If you're using city tap water with chlorine, you should let it sit in an open bucket for a few hours to allow the chemicals to evaporate before using it on your plants. If this isn't possible, there are products at the store that can remove chlorine from tap water, but these may be more expensive than letting water stand overnight, which is usually sufficient!

Weeds

When asked what exactly a weed is, most people think of those pesky plants that pop up in the middle of the garden and make it hard to see the vegetables. However, weeds are any plant that grows where we don't want them to grow – and this may include trees or grass! If this happens, use a hoe to dig them up, making sure to get all of the roots to prevent them from growing back.

Sufficient Lighting

If you want your plants to produce a lot of fruit or vegetables, they need to have access to the right kind of light that's available. This means eight hours per day if they're grown indoors and six hours per day during the winter months when the days are shorter.

Use artificial light, such as fluorescent bulbs, when natural light is harder to access during the winter months.

Pollination

If you've noticed that your plants are full of flowers but few fruits, it could be because they aren't being pollinated. You can help this process by taking a paintbrush or cotton swab and transferring pollen from one flower to another. This will also prevent your plants from producing seeds because these won't grow into vegetables.

Harvesting Your Vegetables

When you've grown an abundance of vegetables, it's time to harvest them. Make sure that the ground isn't wet and that the vegetables are completely dry before picking them. Use a sharp knife to cut the stem of your vegetable from its roots, leaving a small amount in place, so it doesn't damage the plant when you pull it out by hand or using a trowel.

It's important to be gentle with your vegetables because this will prevent them from getting bruised and increase the amount you'll be able to harvest. If they're too delicate, use a spade or hand-fork to dig around them instead of pulling on their stems.

They may look slightly different sizes, but it's important not to pick your vegetables until they've reached maturity because this will ensure that they don't get bitter or rot quickly.

When you're harvesting your vegetables, only pick the ones that are ripe and leave a few to continue growing! This will also help prevent them from falling over because they won't have as much weight at their base. Use a carrier bag or basket so that it's easier to carry your harvest home.

Once you get to the vegetable garden, lay out a large tarp or plastic sheet so that you can lay out your crop, and the vegetables are easy to pick up. This step will prevent them from getting dirty when in storage and make it easier for you if there's rain in the forecast.

What to Do after Your Vegetables Have Been Harvested

When harvesting isn't an issue, it's important to ensure that your vegetables are properly stored to prevent them from rotting. If you live in a cool climate where the temperature often drops below freezing during winter months, use water or sand to fill bags so they don't freeze and crack.

You can also protect your vegetables by covering them with newspapers before putting them in storage because this will help prevent them from getting dirty.

You can also store your vegetables in a garage or cellar if you have one, but make sure it's dry and not too cold! If the ground is particularly wet where they are grown, use sandbags to keep them away from moisture on the floor when harvesting so that they don't rot when you put them away.

If you have a lot of vegetables that need to be stored, use large containers or boxes with lids so there's less chance they'll get damaged. Don't stack too many on top of each other, and be sure to store the most delicate vegetables at the top where heavier items won't squash them.

Fertilizers and Pesticides

If you want to give your vegetables the best chance of growing big and strong, it's important to ensure they have access to nutrients.

You can do this by using fertilizers made for vegetable gardens because these will only contain one type of nutrient rather than a mixture that could burn their roots! Look out for nitrogen-rich manure, seaweed extract, and bone meal to give your vegetable plants the best chance of success.

It's easy to use pesticides in spray form, but this can be wasteful if they're not needed or over-applied when it comes to harvesting time. Instead, try treating individual plants by applying the pesticide directly to their leaves so you can target potential problems without wasting too much.

Greenhouse Garden Maintenance

Once you have your greenhouse, it's important to keep it maintained so that plants can grow as quickly and efficiently as possible!

Every year, clean out all the old plant cuttings from the previous season because these will start to produce mold, which could damage new growth. Don't forget to remove dead leaves before they go rotten, which is a breeding ground for insects and fungus.

Once a year, clean the greenhouse by removing any dirt from surfaces with soapy water. The easiest way is to use old newspapers, which you can throw away after use because they won't leave behind any fibers or lint like a cloth might.

Every month, check your plants for signs of disease or mold because this can spread quickly and cause damage to your plants. If you notice any issues, try treating them as soon as possible otherwise, they could end up killing the *entire crop.*

Every two months, check that all pots have a drainage hole because if water builds up in the bottom, it will become stagnant, which is the perfect breeding ground for disease!

Every three months, check the greenhouse roof to make sure it isn't leaking or buckling because damage like this can cause water to seep through and soak the plants, which could ruin them.

Finally, thoroughly clean your whole greenhouse once per year by washing off any dirt with soapy water, as mentioned before, and then apply a fresh layer of sealant or paint as it may start to need upkeep.

It's easy to grow vegetables in your greenhouse by following some simple guidelines. Whether you're just starting or are an experienced gardener, these tips will help you produce healthy food for yourself and your family with minimal effort on your part. Remember that planning is the most important step, so make sure to plan ahead before planting any crops.

Armed with this knowledge, you should be ready to grow your own vegetables in a greenhouse!

Chapter 9: Growing Fruits

While most hothouses are used to grow vegetables or ornamental plants, there is no reason why you wouldn't be able to cultivate fruit in your greenhouse as well. As with any other plant, it's a question of matching their environment to their native location. You should also consider how much space each fruit plant variety requires to grow and their different nature of sensitivity. This chapter will provide you with a comprehensive guide to which fruit you can grow in your greenhouse, how to plant them and how to take care of them. You will also learn what to watch for in terms of climate change, switch factors to consider, and possible pest infestation before even planting your fruit.

Strawberries

https://unsplash.com/photos/strawberries-in-white-ceramic-bowl-Q5txWuRb6DI

Fruits to Grow in a Greenhouse

The general limitation for growing any fruit in a greenhouse is the size and the temperature. A heated greenhouse can provide a much better environment for growing certain fruit varieties and helps remove limitations set by your climate. Other fruits will thrive in somewhat colder conditions. There are also those that you might even keep outside at the chill of winter while they are in an inactive phase and move them only before they blossom.

If you have a smaller space, you may prefer to cultivate either smaller fruit varieties or keep them in a pot while pruning them frequently so they won't shadow other plants, and you can move around them as well. For some plants, potting won't be an option because they won't be able to reach their full potential, which will cause them to bear smaller fruit or nothing at all.

If you manage to meet the various conditions required by the type of tree you are trying to grow, you can get them to flower and even bear fruit. Despite this, not every species is suitable to grow in a greenhouse. For the best results, it's recommended to opt for varieties that are fairly easy to grow in what is basically an artificial environment. If you have a little bit of experience or are willing to invest a little bit more time, effort, and money, you may be able to try your luck with some hard-to-grow species as well.

Greenhouse Friendly Fruits

The most popular fruit grown in greenhouses are citrus trees, but you don't necessarily have to limit yourself to these. Almost every tropical, subtropical, or Mediterranean fruit will fare well in a greenhouse. The only limitations for these are the height or width some fruit trees may have that would exceed the size of your greenhouse. Remember to pay attention to the average height of the fully grown fruit plant when looking for the species you would like to plant. Fortunately, some of them have dwarf varieties, so you can even try these for smaller spaces or pay more attention to trimming regular trees. Here are some of the best fruits to grow in a greenhouse:

- **Citrus:** Although normal-sized orange and lemon trees grow tall and require a larger space, the appropriate varieties will bear fruit when they reach their maximum height.

- **Fig:** Figs are easy to cultivate in a pot, and you can even plant-train them, so they grow against the wall and take up less space. The only thing you will need to provide them with is plenty of water daily.

- **Strawberries:** As long as they are planted properly, strawberries are easy to take care of in a greenhouse. In fact, after citrus trees, strawberries are the second most popular option for growing in an artificial environment.

- **Goldenberries:** Similar to tomatoes, goldenberries are really easy to grow in a greenhouse. They do have a fair amount of leaves, so they are better suited for larger spaces.

- **Melons:** If you have experience growing vegetables like cucumbers in a greenhouse, you will be able to grow melons as well as they more or less grow under similar conditions.

Fruits that Are Hard to Grow in a Greenhouse

Some fruit has more than one hard-to-meet requirement, which limits or prevents their cultivation in greenhouses. These either need a colder environment to produce flowers and fruit or have special needs in terms of pollination. The former usually go through a natural cycle during the seasons, and unless they are kept under a colder climate for most of the time, they will not thrive. So, you will either have to keep them in large pots and move them in and out a couple of times a year, or save yourself the trouble and leave them outside covered. The case is similar with non-self-pollinating fruit trees that need other plants of the same kind flowering beside them or a high level of insect activity to pollinate, which is sometimes only possible outside of a greenhouse.

Grapes

Here is a list of some fruits that are more difficult to grow in a greenhouse:

- **Peaches:** While you can protect them from most pests, you will still have to watch them vigilantly for any that may have got into the greenhouse. In addition, if the temperatures are not right when the fruit grows, it will never ripen.

- **Nectarines:** Since nectarines are a genetic variation of peaches, the same requirements and possible threats to look out for apply to them.

- **Apricots:** Although they are less sensitive to temperature than peaches or nectarine, apricots need more space to grow. Therefore, you will need to cultivate them in the ground - otherwise, they will only bear smaller fruit.

- **Apples:** The best way to cultivate apple trees in a greenhouse is to move them in from the outside when they are about to blossom. You will need to have at least two different apple trees flowering simultaneously so they can pollinate each other.

- **Grapes:** Some grape varieties tend to be quite sensitive, even in the outside environment. To successfully cultivate them in an artificial one, you will need to select the less sensitive variety and pay special attention to each of its growth phases.

Fruits That are Not Suitable for Greenhouses

Due to space limitations, being overly sensitive to environmental changes, or other needs that can only be met outside a greenhouse, some fruit varieties are generally not recommended to be kept in this environment. If you have space for it and your climate is suitable for them, consider cultivating them outside. Here are some examples of fruit that are not recommended for greenhouse growth:

https://pixabay.com/zh/photos/green-coconuts-kohphangan-island-3681261/

Coconut

- **Coconuts:** Coconut palms are extremely sensitive to cold and pests, have specific pollination requirements, and need a lot of space to grow. Providing all these for even a dwarf coconut palm efficiently enough to produce quality fruit will be too expensive for most home greenhouse owners.

- **Walnuts:** A walnut tree grows tall and requires a lot of space around them. They are also pollinated by other walnuts, which means you will need to have at least two of them flowering in the general vicinity of each other. Plus, even the smallest amount of fertilizer can prevent them from bearing fruit which means you won't be able to keep anything else in your greenhouse.

- **Kiwi:** A very avid climber with large leaves, kiwi can only be grown in a greenhouse if you can keep it under control, so it doesn't shade other plants. However, since this means pruning daily, it's best to stay clear of it.

Tips for Growing Fruit in a Greenhouse

While having a greenhouse is a great way to cultivate fruit plants throughout the entire year, this is only possible if you understand all the factors that may affect your plants' growth. Apart from choosing a properly sized space to grow and produce fruit successfully, there will be a couple of things you will have to pay attention to as well.

Understanding the Climate

Each fruit variety requires a particular environment, and growing them outside of their optimal temperature range will result in a failure to thrive. For this reason, it's crucial to understand what growing climate each plant in your greenhouse needs.

You will have control over the temperatures inside the greenhouse, and you should use this to provide your plants with the environmental conditions they prefer. For example, citrus trees prefer warm temperatures, more so if they are cultivated in a pot, in which they have less soil to serve as an insulator for their roots. Of course, for this to work, you should take into consideration the outside temperatures as well. Learning how many days per year your area has freezing or above-average temperatures during the seasons may take time, but it is imperative to decide which plants will thrive best in your greenhouse.

Living in a generally colder climate, you may be able to prolong the summer for fruit growing outside by moving them into a greenhouse. Keeping fruit plants in pots so you can move them quickly is a viable solution for smaller plants. You can also protect sensitive plants by wrapping them up before the frost, even inside the greenhouse.

If you live in a climate where the temperatures during winter are below the freezing point for an extended period, you will need to ensure that the roots of your trees stay warm and that they don't freeze. It's a good idea to invest in a greenhouse heating system that can protect your sensitive plants. If your plants cool down due to low temperatures, you should also stop watering them when the temperatures drop until you can warm them up to prevent freezing of the roots. Put down a thick layer of mulch, and if the plants are still bearing fruit, cover them with a light blanket.

If you live in a hot climate, you will need to put off fruit planting until the temperatures drop as this will prevent the plants from drying up, the fruit from spoiling, and you can cut down watering costs significantly. However, if you already have some planted, there are a few things you can do to help them survive the heat of the summer. Keeping a thick layer of mulch on the ground can serve as an insulator and even reduce the risks of heat stress. It also traps moisture so the roots will be kept healthy and well-nourished.

Mature plants are more resistant to sunlight than immature ones, so you can place younger ones between the old ones to provide them with some shade. Watering should be done only in the morning to prevent the water from evaporating and use a proper ventilation system to help circulate the air during the hottest hour of the day. Pruning and trimming should be avoided during this period as it may lead to the plants suffering and even death due to their inability to heal.

Planting Different Fruit Plants

When choosing the varieties to produce a year-round supply of fruit, you will have to make several decisions. Certain fruit plants will bear fruit in spring and summer, while others will prefer to produce fruit during the colder months. And since you can't imitate several different climates during one season, you will have to plant your varieties by ensuring their active seasons sync up. You may be able to delay the optimal seasons by cooling or heating, but this may affect your other plants, which can suffer and fail to thrive.

Fruit trees grown in the ground are usually larger, and they often produce an abundance of leaves as well. Consequently, their size will eventually make moving them or planting around them difficult. They will shade everything and won't give you enough space to reorganize your greenhouse either. The depth of their roots will also make it impossible to install weed protection, which will lead to weeds spreading through the entire space. For this reason, it's advisable to have all your fruit plants in pots (even the trees) and trim them frequently so they will be easy to move around. Potting is particularly a good solution if you are planning to keep citrus plants throughout the year. Though they will produce less fruit due to their lack of extensive branching, they will be simple to move outside during the summer - which is something you will absolutely have to do.

https://unsplash.com/photos/person-picking-orange-fruit-xEPMg4qfjOs

Oranges

Pollination is another factor to be considered when choosing fruit plants. Even though they are self-pollinating plants, most of them will need cross-pollination, insect activity, or wind to get pollinated. Depending on the fruit varieties you have planted, you will have to perform manual pollination or attract insects into your greenhouse. For the cross-pollinating varieties, you will need to keep at least two different plants next to each other for them to be able to bear fruit.

Maintaining Soil and Fertilizing

After the climate, the most important factor determining whether your fruit plants will thrive or not will be the soil you have planted them in. Planting them in organic soil is always a good idea, as this type is full of all the nutrients and minerals that your plants will need. Plus, the natural ingredients provide better insulation for the roots of plants during the winter. Leaf compost and garden soil mixture are usually the most suitable for these purposes. Aside from these, feel free to use any organic waste you produce in your home and mix it into the soil you use in the greenhouse. Limiting the number of pesticides and eradicating pests also helps to keep the soil fertile and the roots healthier.

Because the same varieties use the same nutrients, it's not a good idea to plant the same fruit plants in the same spot in your greenhouse year after year. Try rotating them each year so the soil has enough time to regenerate the nutrients used up the previous year. Keep the soil loose most of the time so that the water can carry the nutrients deep into the ground.

When the substrate becomes devoid of nutrients, you will have to turn to fertilizers to keep nourishing your fruit plants. You should use natural fertilizers and only after analyzing the soil's mineral content. Knowing what the soil lacks will help you determine the exact type of fertilizer you will need for your soil and the amount you should use in it.

The Importance of Irrigation

Irrigation will be another crucial part of taking care of your fruit plants. Depending on whether you keep the majority of your plants potted or in the ground, you will need to employ different watering strategies. A smaller amount of soil will always dry out faster, which will mean more frequent watering. On the other hand, roots of plants growing in open ground can reach much further, so even if the upper part of the soil is dehydrated, they will still be able to find moisture. This will keep them nourished for longer, and they will need less frequent watering.

Most fruit plants like colder, moist soils when they are in the active growth phase, so it's a good idea to install a drip irrigation system that can provide them with a small amount of water constantly. It's a far more economical solution than manually watering them during drought season, and it allows for a more even water distribution. As the plants develop stronger roots, they will need less and less water.

Keep in mind that each fruit variety has its own water requirements, and try to set up your irrigation system in a way that suits your plants the best. You can learn how the plants use the water by measuring how much time it takes for the upper part of the soil to dry out after each watering. If you can, try watering them with rainwater or at least water with some lime.

Moving, Root Care, and Pruning

For potted fruit plants, you will need to change their soil every 1-2 years. A fresh soil will provide them with more nutrients and more space - which is particularly helpful if they are still growing. When they have stopped growing, you can stop changing the entire soil, and you will only need to replace its surface each year. Make sure you place at least 2 inches of compost and fertilizer mixture on the top of the rootage.

After a while, you may notice some decline in the health of your plant. In this case, you will need to replace the entire soil once again. When doing this, make sure you use a disinfected tool and remove 2-4 inches of the side roots but keep the root ball intact. Try trimming the roots during this process so they will use less soil - and you won't have to repeat the replanting again for years to come.

Pruning fruit plants is necessary for ensuring appropriate fruit development. Without it, the growing plants would only put all their energy into growing the new structures and will fail to bear fruit. The best time to do this is when the plants go into a vegetative state since there will be less chance of damaging any vital part of the plant. Even then, you should perform the pruning with a sharp and clean tool to avoid spreading damaging microorganisms through cuts.

Keeping Your Fruit Plants Pest-Free

Pests are an inevitable part of gardening, and you won't be able to avoid them in your greenhouse either. Some pests will be easier to control, while others will require more intense monitoring and critical steps to eradicate.

The most common pests you may encounter in your greenhouse are:

- Sap-feeding insects
- Mites
- Pollen feeders
- Caterpillars and slugs

It's advisable to monitor these throughout the entire year with sticky cards so you can catch them if they begin to spread immediately. Place the cards near the most sensitive plants and keep replacing them weekly, especially during the summer when the pests show the most activity. Should you notice any plants infested with small animals, spray them with insecticidal soaps liberally by coating the underside of the leaves and stems too. Repeat the treatment every 5-7 days until the pests are gone.

Most small pests and their larvae will disappear after 1-2 weeks. To control scale insects, you may need to use neem oil applied similarly, but even they should be gone after 10-12 days. Caterpillars and slugs should be hand-picked, as you would need more chemicals to kill them, but that could also damage your plants.

Chapter 10: Growing Herbs

If you think you will never be able to grow herbs in your garden because of extremes in cold or hot weather, then let us assure you that it is indeed possible. A greenhouse can help you grow a thriving herb garden at your home.

Herbs are appreciated for the aroma and taste they bring to our favorite dishes. They tend to enhance the taste of any dish you can think of, not to mention the wide array of medicinal properties they possess.

Greenhouse gardening gives you the ability to grow your own fruit and vegetables and enables you to grow herbs that cannot otherwise withstand harsh weather. It provides you with a controlled artificial environment to grow fragile plants and herbs. Using a greenhouse can prolong the growing season for you, and it also allows you to grow a wide range of plants in your own garden.

Thanks to its customizable settings that allow you to control the environment, you can grow hundreds of different types of herbs in your greenhouse. Greenhouse gardeners find it extremely easy to grow hardy herbs in the greenhouse rather than in soil or pots.

What Herbs Need to Thrive

Moisture

It is extremely important to set up your greenhouse before you start planting herbs. As herbs are quite sensitive, the main reason they fail is due to the lack of moisture. It is essential to install an automatic misting system in your greenhouse to ensure that your plants' moisture needs are being met. The automatic supply can provide your herbs with an adequate supply of water regularly to help them thrive. This way, your herbs will be able to grow steadily without you having to worry about forgetting or overdoing them.

Shade

The system of shading the plants in your greenhouse is also essential. If you plan to add herbs to your greenhouse garden, you may want to consider not getting a roof completely made of glass. This is because most, if not all, herbs require shading from direct sunlight. If you already own a greenhouse with a glass roof, then you may want to consider creating a DIY shade system with hooks and Velcro. It will help you manage the shading needs of your plants.

Space

It is essential to have enough space in your greenhouse to allow your herbs to grow. For example, a large plant like Rosemary will need a lot of space. You should also try your best to plant similar herbs together so that you can match their moisture and shade requirements.

Sunlight

Another factor to consider is how much light your herb needs to thrive, and that can range from needing a lot of light to needing very little. These differences are why you should plant similar herbs together to ensure that their lighting needs are met.

Herbs that Can Thrive in a Greenhouse

All herbs have different needs and requirements. It is important to do proper research before going ahead with planting your herbs. Take the time to ensure that you have all the tools you need to build a favorable environment for the herbs you're going to plant. Let's take a look at the best herbs that can thrive in a greenhouse.

Oregano

Oregano is one of the most well-known herbs that you can grow in your own greenhouse and can be grown in your garden under the right conditions. Being a perennial herb, it loves light and warmth – and why you will need a lot of or adequate sunlight to make this plant grow. Under the right circumstances and with enough light, you will have your oregano growing in no time!

Mint

Mint is one of the most loved herbs of all time. You can use it in your drinks, foods, and even desserts! What makes this herb even better is that it can grow anywhere it's planted, making it a great herb to grow indoors. You can grow it in your own kitchen if you don't have the space in your greenhouse. It will take over the containers, pots, and grow practically anywhere! With its wide array of uses, this herb will make for a wonderful addition to your garden.

Parsley

Parsley loves the sunshine too and thrives best where there's adequate light for it to grow. You can use a grow lamp to provide the essential light it needs. Provided there's enough light in your greenhouse for this herb to grow, you will have a wonderful addition to your variety!

Dill

Dill is a great herb used to make pickles, garnish on soups, and even makes an amazing addition to your salad. You can also use it to add flavor to your fish. This wonderful herb is grown in cold weather and doesn't require much light. Under the right conditions, it will thrive.

Chives

Chives are an extremely delicious herb to grow. It does great in well-draining soil that is spacious enough for it to grow, provided it has the amount of sunlight it needs. Chives can be used for garnishing purposes, and they can also be used in a salad.

Lemon Grass

If you're a beginner, then lemongrass is the perfect herb to start with. This herb requires a good amount of sunlight, so it should be placed with that in mind – or you can provide it with the light it needs to grow through a grow lamp. Besides its need for light, it is pretty easy to grow, develops pretty quickly, tastes wonderful, and even has a delicious smell.

Thyme

Thyme is the herb that can seriously add the missing flavor to your dish. With its intense and delicious aroma, it will enhance your meals. Moreover, it does not need that much sunlight. Indirect sunlight is great for it, and it does not even require much water. Therefore, you don't need to look after it that much. This also makes for an amazing herb to grow for beginners.

https://pixabay.com/zh/photos/thyme-medicinal-herb-cook-seasoning-2854035/

Chervil

Chervil is usually used in French cuisines, so if you're looking to take your French cuisine game to the next level, try adding chervil to your garden. This herb is not that common. However, it's pretty simple to grow. This plant requires low temperature, moist soil, and indirect sunlight. This low-maintenance plant could make a wonderful addition to your greenhouse.

Rosemary

If you live in a comparatively hotter area, then rosemary is the herb for you. This plant thrives in adequate light and humidity. However, it will need to be tended more frequently than the other herbs. It needs to be watered using the deep watering method. You may also need to spritz it often to create an adequately humid environment.

How to Care for Your Herbs

It is important to take good care of your plants to keep them healthy and safe from bug infestations or diseases.

Choose Healthy Herbs to Plant

It is important for the health of your entire herb garden to plant healthy herbs by making sure that they are free from any infestations or diseases. You should plant your herbs in the right environment to allow them to grow to their full potential healthily. Recognize your plants' needs and see if it thrives in moist or dry weather, more or less light, etc.

Give Your Herbs Some Space

Your herbs require space to grow. It is essential for you not to overcrowd your herbs and give them enough room to help them grow to their full potential.

Fertilize

You should ensure that your plants' nutrients are not deficient, as this can stunt their growth. Adding an organic fertilizer to the soil of your herb garden can help them get the nutrients they need. It is also important to make sure that their moisture needs are met.

Basic Needs

Ensure that your plants' basic needs, such as the moisture level, light, shading, etc., are all being met as this can seriously affect their growth.

Prune

It is important to harvest your herbs regularly. This will help you get rid of any infected herb and provide you with a better, healthier plant. Harvesting will also help you get rid of its flowers, as the growth of flowers gives them the signal to die for the season.

https://unsplash.com/photos/man-in-white-long-sleeve-shirt-and-blue-denim-jeans-sitting-on-brown-wooden-fence-during-wz3ijPHvL54

What Soil or Fertilizer Should Be Used for Your Herb Garden?

It is possible that your herb garden may not need that much fertilizer; still, fertilizer can help meet your herbs' nutrient requirements organically. Moreover, if you're growing your herbs in a container, they're going to need more care. The container-grown plants need a lot of nutrients as they grow. These nutrients are also expelled from the container when these plants are watered. You should know that potted plants are quicker to dry out than plants planted in soil. Due to all these reasons, you should definitely consider getting a fertilizer to fulfill your plants' needs.

There are many options for organic fertilizers that you can use for your greenhouse garden to benefit your plants with the essential nutrients they need. There are many types of fertilizers that you can use for your plants. A time-release organic fertilizer is used before you plant your plants. This way, your plants are planted in already nutrient-rich soil. You can also use liquid fertilizers to help your herbs retain their vibrant look, especially if they have started to look weaker or lose color. However, it is important not to over-fertilize your herbs as this can lead to more growth than you can handle, and consequently, it will dilute their flavor and aroma.

If you live in a cold climate, it is essential for you not to fertilize your herbs late in the growing season. This is because fertilizing them in the late season will make them grow rapidly, whereas you want their growth to slow down to extend the growing season. This is essential to protect your plants in winter as they have shallow roots that can easily get destroyed in frost weather. In cold weather, a layer of mulch can keep your herbs warm. You can use oak leaves, evergreen boughs, or straw as organic mulch for your garden around the base of each plant. You should only remove mulch in spring after your plant starts to grow. However, it is important to avoid using mushy mulches as they can cause your plants to rot.

How to Deal with Pests or Issues That Might Arise

Getting your plants attacked by a pest invasion is every gardener's worst nightmare. It is important to take precautionary measures to keep your herbs safe from pests. Mostly, the essential oils that the herbs contain act as insect repellent. However, some pests may still be able to invade your herb garden. Fortunately, most of these pests do not cause any major harm to your plants. Still, it is helpful to recognize the pests that you should be aware of:

Aphids

Aphids are notorious for feasting on the young leaves and may cause the foliage to curl when there are many of them. These pests are more common in rapidly growing herbs. The best way to get rid of aphids is to use horticultural soaps or neem oil on them.

Spider Mites

If your herb requires a hot and dry climate, you should know that it is also favorable for spider mites. These pests are found under the herb leaves. However, getting rid of them is fairly easy. All you have to do is use a high-pressure water hose, and they'll come right off. Regularly watering your plants will also help.

Parsley Worms

Not all pests are bad. Parsley worms, also called Black Swallowtail caterpillars, may feast on dill, parsley, or fennel. However, they also turn into beautiful butterflies. If you can, spare these bugs and separate them from the rest of the vegetation by providing it with enough parsley to feed on.

Some diseases affect herbs that you need to be aware of as well. Most of these diseases thrive in wet soil. Wet soil may increase the chances of fungal diseases like fusarium root rot in plants. This disease may cause your herbs to collapse, starting with the appearance of brown streaks on the plant's stems. Another disease, the rust plague, attacks mint herbs. It causes the underside of the mint leaves to turn rusty orange. To prevent these diseases, it is important to maintain a proper sanitation system in your greenhouse garden. You should immediately remove any affected plant and regularly prune your plants. Raising beds can also decrease the chances of diseases, and watering it in the morning to allow it to dry will also lessen the risk of fungal diseases.

To protect your plants from pests, pest control materials called bio-rationals are used. They are not as toxic as the other pest controls and are not as harmful to the environment since they have short residual properties. However, the bio-rationals take longer to control the pests. It is important to note that even though some insecticides are licensed to be used on herbs, there is a possibility that they may not have been tested on herbs. This is why as a greenhouse gardener, you should inform yourself of the safe insecticides and pest control materials that you're using for your herbs.

Growing herbs can make for a wonderful addition to your greenhouse garden. It will not only give you access to these delicious and aromatic plants all year long, but it will also improve the aesthetics of your greenhouse. Herbs have numerous culinary and medicinal benefits, making them super useful to have in and around your home. Most of these herbs are not even difficult to maintain and are fairly easy to grow. It is important to take care of your plants' needs, including light exposure, moisture level, and shading to help them grow. To make things easier for yourself, you should try to plant similar herbs together so that you can provide them with a similar environment to help them survive. When it comes to fulfilling the nutritional needs of your plants, it is important to add fertilizer to the soil to ensure that it is getting all the essential nutrients.

You should also try your best to take precautionary measures like regular sanitation to prevent the risk of your plant catching a disease or pest infestation. Plant diseases and infestations in an enclosed environment can spread rapidly. This is why it is important to regularly prune your plants and nip the evil in the bud as soon as you find any symptoms of diseases or infestation. Other than that, growing herbs in your greenhouse can prove to be an absolute treat. With these wonderful aromatic herbs around all the time, you can easily add extra flavor to your dishes, make tasty beverages, and even garnish them on your soups and salads. Herbs will definitely make for a great addition to your greenhouse garden.

Chapter 11: Growing Flowers

There is a huge variety of flowers that you can grow in your greenhouse. Some of the most common flowers to grow in your greenhouse are Fuchsia, Primula, Chrysanthemum, Carnation, Cineraria, etc. However, this is not all. There is a wide range of beautiful and easy-to-grow flowers that are waiting to be discovered in your greenhouse garden. You will have to consider the space you have in your garden before choosing a certain type of flower to keep your greenhouse from getting overcrowded. There are many wonderful and uncommon flowers out there that you can grow. Unlike herbs, flowers are much easier to grow from seeds. You can also ask for a cutting of the plant you like from your friends or someone in your neighborhood. However, first things first, why should you consider growing flowers in your greenhouse anyway? Let's find out!

Why You Should Grow Flowers in Your Greenhouse

You must be wondering why you would ever plant flowers in your greenhouse rather than in your garden or pots. There are numerous reasons why. Here are a few:

Protection

A greenhouse provides your plants with the protection they need. This is why plants have a better chance of survival in your greenhouse garden. The greenhouse also protects these flowers from outside dangers of getting attacked by deer, rabbits, etc. Flowers are also more vulnerable to diseases when they're outside than when they are in a greenhouse.

Fulfills the Needs of These Plants

Moreover, gardeners try their best to provide a favorable environment for their plants and make sure that all their needs are being met. No plant is the same. Each flower has different needs. The plants have a better chance of having their needs fulfilled at a greenhouse as you can control the temperature, moisture level, and the light these plants receive. As these flowers need light to survive, the greenhouse amplifies the light for these plants to facilitate photosynthesis. This also extends the growing season and stabilizes plant growth.

Decreases the Risk of Pests or Diseases

The greenhouse can minimize the risk of pests or disease outbreaks as it offers you the ability to control the environment and also helps you to avoid using toxic chemicals or pest control. Your greenhouse also reduces the risk of diseases such as blight or other fungal diseases as the growing conditions there are less favorable for the fungi to reach and infect your plants.

Flowers to Grow in Your Greenhouse

Now that you know the benefits of planting your flowers in a greenhouse rather than outside, let us look at some of the flowers you can grow.

Geraniums

Geraniums are adored for their appearance as they have beautiful flower clusters and ornamental leaves. When it comes to planting Geraniums in your garden, you must know that they have plenty of benefits besides being beautiful. These flowers are known for their antibacterial characteristics and for their ability to reduce stress levels. Moreover, as a gardener, you will appreciate how extremely low maintenance these plants are. You can grow these flowers in your greenhouse in the winter as well. Keep in mind that the crates or pots you're planting them in should be sterilized to avoid the risk of any bacterial infections. To keep them growing, fresh, and free of diseases such as foliar disease, make sure to spritz them with distilled water every morning.

Flowering Maple

Flowering maples are easy to grow and have maple-like leaves - which is essentially the reason why they're named the flowering maple - and have bell-like flowers that resemble mallow. These hardy evergreen shrubs can grow up to four feet in height and never stop blooming, considering they're kept in the right environment.

Pansies

These bright and beautiful flowers are enough to light up your greenhouse garden and add a cheery feeling to the overall vibe of your greenhouse. Moreover, these plants can grow anywhere, even in flower beds where no plant was before. Pansies can be bought as seedlings or can also be started from seeds. The flowers contain a fine and frilly texture that makes them look oh-so-fancy. The modern hybrid versions of pansies can adjust to heat as compared to those in the past. They bloom the best in the presence of Tulips and Daffodils. However, as pansies are biennials, they may not bloom until their second year, when grown from seeds.

Lipstick Plant

Lipstick plants are attractive, eye-catching flowers that have long stems, waxy leaves, and red flowers. The lipstick plant, as the name suggests, is quite delicate and needs a lot of attention. Lipstick plant leaves must be kept away from direct sunlight, and you should prevent water from falling on them. It also doesn't thrive in dry air, wet soil in the winter season, and cold droughts.

Coralberry

The coralberry has glossy leaves and aromatic pale pink or white flowers, which then turn into berries. You must keep your coralberries cool in winter and prune back in early spring.

How to Plant Your Flowers in the Greenhouse

You can either plant your flowers in the soil, pots, or containers. You can even plant your flowers in buckets, grow bags or even whiskey barrels! This will help you save space in your garden and add to the aesthetic value of your greenhouse garden. You can grow any plant in your containers or pots, including Fuchsias, Pansies, Petunias, Geraniums, Roses, Candytufts, Alyssum, etc. The pots or crates you use must have drainage holes to release any excess water. Once you have thought of the plants you want to grow in your containers and pots, you must carefully consider the needs of your plants. Whether you decide to plant your plants in a pot or a crate, you must make sure they have enough space, time, and all their basic needs provided to them.

Space

It is important to understand how big your plant will potentially grow and if the pot or container that you've chosen will be enough for it to bloom to its full capacity. Dwarf plants are small by nature, so it is easier to grow them in pots and containers.

Water

It is important to keep a check on the water requirements of your plants as their needs are different from the plants that are grown in soil. As the potting mix is less dense than soil, its capacity to hold water is restricted. However, it is important to note the water needs of each plant to ensure that it does not kill them. You can use a digital moisture meter to ensure that your plant's water needs are being met.

Sunlight

Make sure that your pots or container crates are placed where they get the essential sunlight required for their proper growth.

If you're wondering how to plant your flowers in pots, here are a few guidelines.

First, you must sterilize your pot to ensure it's free of bacteria to avoid getting any diseases. Then, you must dampen the potting mix and partially fill your pot or container with it. Then, plant your flowers in the container once it's prepared. If your plant is rootbound, make sure to loosen the roots before you start planting. Then, add soil to the container and pack it lightly around the plant. Then add your mulch or fertilizer on top to help retain the water.

What Soil and Fertilizer Should You Use?

If you are planting your flowers in a pot, you have various soil and fertilizers available for your plants.

Potting Mix

A potting mix can help your plants thrive as this is better for them than garden soil because it can compact easily. Moreover, garden soil may also have weed seeds, some other critters, and pests that you would not want to have in your pot or crate. A potting mix contains organic material that can hold essential water and nutrients to provide your flowers with the nutrients they need. You can even make your potting mix with mature compost, topsoil, and perlite.

Mulch

Adding mulch to the base of your flowers or on the top of containers that you've planted your flowers in will allow you to retain the moisture and nutrients that the flowers need. Moreover, it will also help it stay moisturized on hotter days. The nutrients your plants receive from the mulch will be released through the soil as it is watered. This is why it is important to keep replacing the mulch from time to time.

Fertilizers

The fertilizer adds the additional nutrients that may be lacking in your plants' soil. The fertilizers make up for the deficiencies in the soil and fulfill their nutritional needs. Liquid organic fertilizers like fish emulsion and kelp meal offer the plants nitrogen, phosphorus, and potassium, which may be missing from the soil. You must always opt for an organic fertilizer rather than a synthetic fertilizer as it is healthier and will not burn your flowers. Make sure that you fertilize your plants at the right time. In potted plants, it is easier to add fertilizer twice a week.

Take Care of Your Plants against Pests and Diseases

Caution is always advisable. It is important to take preventative measures to ensure that no pests have infested your flowers. When you buy your plants or seeds, make sure that they are free of pests and diseases. Then, wash them before planting them in the soil or pots. You must make sure that your pots or crates are clean, and you should also wash your hands before planting your flowers. If any of your plants are infected, get rid of the infected part or, if most of its leaves are affected, then get rid of it completely.

Here Are Some Ways to Ensure That Your Plants Are Disease-Free

Keep your Greenhouse Tidy

Keeping your greenhouse clean will help you prevent all sorts of diseases and pests from attacking your beautiful garden. It is important to deep clean your greenhouse garden once a year to ensure no pests are hiding out in the pots or the containers. You must thoroughly clean your greenhouse, including the windows, surfaces, and floors. This will keep your greenhouse fresh and free of any threat of pests.

Check Your Plants for Pests

It is important to inspect your plants regularly. Check them every day for any possible infestations and see if the underside of the leaves has many bugs, such as aphids or spider mites attached to them. It is also usually the place where the bugs hide their eggs. It is also important to check them before bringing them into your greenhouse as they can be the potential post carriers that can affect other plants as well. The pests thrive in the warm and enclosed environment of the greenhouse and breed quickly in warmth.

Sterilize Your Tools

You should sterilize and disinfect your gardening tools regularly as transporting them through your lawn, flower beds, and shed can carry pests with them into your greenhouse through the soil outside or any other infected plants. This is why you should be extra careful when it comes to your tools and deep clean them once in a while to ensure that no pest enters your greenhouse through using them there.

Use Insect Catchers

While you can minimize the risk of pests attacking your plants, it is extremely difficult to get rid of them completely. This is why you must try to restrict the insects from coming into your house and catch them at the entrance. You can use spider sprays, wasp traps, and flypapers to keep these bugs in control. You can also use netting to keep the insects from entering your greenhouse while maintaining good ventilation throughout your greenhouse. Hanging a net across your windows, doors, and other ventilation points can help you keep the pests out and away from your beautiful flowers.

Expose the Pots Out to Heat

You can move your plants outside when the greenhouse becomes too hot and dry. Dry heat can cause spider mites to increase rapidly. This is why you must keep your greenhouse humid to avoid these pests. Taking them out will help them cool down and will also reduce any spider mites build-up on the plants. You can also wet the floor with water to keep the air humidified.

Rotate Crops

If you plant the flowers in the soil rather than in pots or crates, you must try to avoid pest invasion through crop rotation as this prevents the build-up of pests that may infect a certain type of plant.

Potting Soil

Potting soil is better than regular soil as it comes free of insects and pests. Potting them in the potting mix will not only provide your plants with essential nutrients but will also prevent the pests from attacking them.

Freeze the Pests

If you're tired of pests and feel that your greenhouse is completely infested, then you may freeze the pests. This can be done by allowing the greenhouse to reach a freezing temperature to kill all the bugs as they normally thrive in hot and dry weather. During the winter season, you can open all doors and windows of your greenhouse to make your greenhouse chilly for a day or two. This will cause any pests and larvae to die. Make sure you protect your tropical plants during this period as they may not survive this; consider blankets. Still, you may lose some plants.

Use Organic Pest Control

There are plenty of organic pest controls that you can use to get rid of pests. Bugs like whiteflies and spider mites can be dealt with through organic alternatives. You can introduce another bug or reptile that feeds on a certain colony of pests to control them. Once the pest is eliminated, the other organism will be eliminated too. You should learn what sort of pests or diseases your plants have and then buy the relevant pest control to manage them. There are many organic pest control options on the market as well. Pests like aphids and spider mites can spread diseases, and this is why you must take preventive measures to keep them in check.

Flowers will make for a wonderful addition to your greenhouse with their amazing qualities and benefits. There are various flowers that you can plant in your greenhouse, including pansies, chrysanthemums, Lipstick plants, etc. Overall, the flowers will enhance the aesthetic value of your greenhouse with their wonderful presence and many benefits! It is important to understand your plants' needs before you go for them. Also, if you lack space in your greenhouse, you can plant your flowers in pots or crates. However, you will need to make sure that the pots have enough space for the plant to grow and that its other needs are being met. You must also take care of the pests and diseases that may infect your flowers.

Chapter 12: Gardening Calendar

Now that you have grasped all the important aspects of greenhouse gardening you want to know, this last chapter gives you suggestions for the types of vegetables, herbs, fruit, or flowers you can plant each month. It also outlines the harvesting periods of different crops in your greenhouse garden. Additionally, it highlights the significance of a planting schedule for your garden.

Factors to Consider When Growing Your Food

There are many benefits you can get from growing your food in a greenhouse. With a greenhouse, you can grow a variety of crops all year round. To succeed in this endeavor, you must consider two fundamental factors: the length of the day and the temperature. When determining what to plant and when to plant it, the length of the day is probably the most important factor to consider.

You must understand the average day lengths during different seasons of the year if you do not intend to use supplemental lighting. Particular seasons have longer days, while others are relatively short. Longer days provide sufficient light to enhance plant growth, but the growth significantly slows down when the days become shorter. Therefore, you must choose plants that are appropriate for winter or summer cropping. For instance, certain plants like kale and spinach can do well throughout the winter.

If you plan your planting schedule according to temperature, day length, and selecting the ideal crops, you are likely to enjoy an all-year-round harvest of vegetables. The following is a rough draft schedule that can give insight into different crops you can plant if you live in the northern region, where temperatures are usually low.

February

February often gives us 10 hours of daylight in different places. This means that you can seed new crops without any need to use supplemental lighting. This is also the time to begin seeding cold-tolerant crops like kale, lettuce, beets, radishes, peas, and carrots. It's also the time for seeding long-term crops that love warm temperatures like peppers, eggplant, and tomatoes. These crops don't tolerate cold weather, and they usually take up to 150 days to mature.

You must give your crops sufficient time to grow and ripen under warm conditions. Warm temperatures are appropriate for a variety of plants that include herbs, flowers, carrots, spinach, and others. February is also an ideal month to promote the sprouting of potatoes before growing them. If you want, you can plant your seeds inside the greenhouse then transplant them later. This process is also known as chitting.

March/April

During these months, the daylight will lengthen, and crops in the greenhouse begin to grow quickly; this is the time to seed warm-season plants with shorter maturity days like beans, cucumbers, basil, and squash. You must start by harvesting crops that are cold-tolerant and replace them. The other thing you must know is that temperature fluctuations can cause the greenhouse to overheat. You should ventilate your greenhouse to moderate the temperature and humidity levels. It is essential to open the vents to maintain low levels of humidity to prevent plant diseases.

The other types of crops you can grow include peas, beans, and broadleaf vegetables. You must do your research about crops that do well when temperatures are warm. It is a good idea to plant seeds that germinate quickly. Plants with shorter maturity days are appropriate for your greenhouse garden. In short, you must plant any crop you want in your garden as long as you are certain that it will reach maturity.

May

May is characterized by longer days and warmer nights which promote faster growth of plants in your greenhouse. During this period, you are likely to harvest several crops, including spinach, kale, lettuce, and peas. This is also the time you can start planting transplants that are cold tolerant, like cabbage, broccoli, and cauliflower, when the night temperature is above 45 degrees. You can also add warm-season plants like peppers, tomatoes, and eggplants.

When you want to grow vegetables, you can consider beetroot since it is very easy to grow. It can easily germinate and does not require a lot of attention and care. Dwarf French beans are also ideal for planting during this period since they need warmth. May is the month to grow other plants like sweetcorn and buttery corn. You must give these plants time to grow and ripen. As you can see, some plants that do well in cold weather conditions must be planted in May in your greenhouse.

June/July

This is a very hot time, especially if you live in the northern region. Your greenhouse is likely to be hot inside, and you will need an effective cooling system to moderate the temperature. The plants that thrive during this period include eggplants, tomatoes, and peppers. You still need to constantly check the temperature in your greenhouse to prevent overheating. It is vital to ensure quality ventilation and sufficient humidity to prevent issues like plant wilting.

Peas can grow well in a greenhouse during this period when the temperatures are high. You can also consider other crops that do well under warm conditions and check their maturity period. Feel free to try different crops in your greenhouse to come up with the best. High temperatures are good for specific crops, but you must be careful to ensure that they get sufficient water.

August/September

This is the ideal time to begin planting your winter garden. The days will begin to shorten, and your plants will grow slowly if you do not provide supplemental lighting. To get a good winter harvest, you must plant early so that most plants are close to maturity around November and December. The plants often go into semi-hibernation as slow growth ticks. The good thing is that you can still enjoy a constant harvest of winter crops even if there is very slow growth.

You need to move all the potted plants into your greenhouse. If you move the plants into the greenhouse, other long-term plants like peppers, tomatoes, figs, and citrus can do well in winter. Some can go for three years producing offspring. Cabbage and other resistant vegetables also grow well during this time of the year. These plants can only experience slow growth, but they are not severely affected by elements like temperature changes. You should make sure the plants get favorable temperatures and water supply.

In some cases, September signals the arrival of spring, and your greenhouse garden will begin to show signs of life. This is the time you should begin planting spring crops. It is essential to remove older plants to create room for new plants. You can dig in the old green plants to create compost. However, this should not stop you from planting new crops in the spaces you clear.

You can consider several crops for spring – try lettuce, peas, beans, broccoli, beetroot, celery, carrots, and potatoes. You can also grow spring onions and spinach during this period since these plants usually take longer to reach maturity. This is also the time to plant strawberries, so they will give you fresh crops when they ripen. You must keep weeds at bay since they can disturb the growth of your crop. When the temperature gets warm, weeds will also start growing fast.

October

If you live in the northern regions, the temperatures begin to shorten in October. Since your winter plants are already planted, they can continue to thrive under the prevailing conditions. October still provides sufficient light that can allow you to start crops with very short cycles like radishes. These only need about 20 to 30 days to mature. You can also consider planting crops with a slow growth rate throughout the winter so they will be ready at the end of the season.

Plants like lettuce, spinach, and kale can be planted in October so that they will have ample time to germinate. They will survive as small plants during the winter period and will experience rapid growth when days begin to lengthen as the summer season starts. Other crops you can plant throughout winter include herbs like parsley, chives, dill, and basil. Other spring crops you can plant during this period include onions and cauliflowers. These are not the only crops you can plant in your greenhouse. You should consider other factors like the type of soil in your area to determine the ideal crops to grow.

November/December/January

These months are great periods to rest while you harvest other plants at the same time. Plants that are mature like kale, carrots, and spinach should be harvested during this period. This is also the time to perform other activities like winter pruning fruit trees, reading different notes, and planning for next season. You can use supplemental light to ensure that plant growth does not slow down.

Root vegetables and other leafy greens can thrive in your greenhouse during winter with little supplemental light. Toward the end of the month, it is vital to plant salad crops or other varieties you may think of. While you will be harvesting other crops from your greenhouse, do not forget to add all unwanted leaves to your compost. This is the appropriate time for composting as you prepare for a new cropping season. The advantage of organic manure is that it is environmentally friendly compared to artificial fertilizers and chemicals. This will also conserve your soil and prevent issues like plant diseases.

You can also use compost to warm the soil in a bid to prevent the young plants or seeds from being chilled. This can affect germination if the soil temperatures are very low. It also provides different types of nutrients required for plant growth.

When to Harvest Your Crops

You must harvest your crops when they are ripe and ready to ensure high-quality produce. You should check the instructions on the package of the seeds you buy. Some plants have different maturity periods, and others are seasonal. You must get this information before you decide to plant any crop in your garden. If you want to buy seedlings, you must consult an agronomist in your area to ensure that you make the right decision. You can take a sample of your soil to a lab, where experts can examine it. They will also advise you on different types of crops you can grow in your greenhouse garden.

Another important aspect you should consider is that you need to rotate the crops in your garden. For instance, you can include three or four different crops that you can rotate every year in your greenhouse garden. If you harvest a crop after 90 days, plant a different one, and it will be ready after the same period or more. This means that you can enjoy all-year-round cropping, including various crops.

The Value of a Planting Schedule

It is important to have a planting schedule if you want to realize your greenhouse farming goals. A schedule is vital since it acts like a guideline that provides you with the directions you should follow when you undertake various activities related to greenhouse gardening. There is no strict outline to follow when you develop your planting schedule. However, make sure you follow it to give your crops sufficient growing time. Since you know your needs, you can design any plan that suits them! It is a good idea to experiment with different things to be able to develop your knowledge of greenhouse agriculture.

The main advantage of greenhouse farming is that it promotes all-year-round farming regardless of different weather elements and seasons. However, it is essential to create a calendar for your gardening activities. It should determine the type of plants to grow at a specific period and outline the harvesting time for each crop. To succeed in your endeavor, you must have a proper schedule.

Conclusion

If you are a novice in greenhouse gardening, you should now have accurate knowledge about all the elements that can significantly contribute to your success. As you have observed in this informative book, it is important to understand the basics of greenhouse gardening before you begin your journey in horticulture. You need to choose the right frame for your greenhouse and create a structure that best suits your needs. This book provides a step-by-step guide on how to begin greenhouse gardening.

Another important aspect of this unique book is that it gives insight into what you need to know about irrigation systems and maintaining the appropriate temperature and humidity. Depending on your greenhouse garden type and your soil texture, you need to get an appropriate irrigation system to suit your needs. This book offers all the details you'll need to make the right decision on watering systems to enhance productivity. As you have realized above, there are several types of irrigation systems, and they are designed to suit the needs of different farmers. The good thing is that all the crucial details have been covered. Your ultimate choice of irrigation system will be a matter of personal preference.

This book is a quite useful tool that can help you on your journey toward success in greenhouse gardening. We've provided guidance on dealing with other important issues that can affect the quality of your crops and yield, such as ventilation and lighting. Many people are unsuccessful at greenhouse gardening due to a lack of knowledge regarding proper lighting for their greenhouses. This book is particularly valuable since it provides information about growing different types of crops in your garden. As mentioned in this book, a greenhouse garden is specifically meant for horticultural produce like vegetables, fruit, flowers, and other fresh items.

The success of your greenhouse garden depends on the type of crops you choose. As you have learned in this book, different factors like the soil type and the size of your greenhouse garden play a crucial role in determining the ideal plants to choose. It is essential to consult a professional agronomist before choosing the crops to plant. This section is explained in detail and forms the crux of the book. To avoid wasting time planting crops that may not be compatible with your greenhouse and soil, it's best to bear in mind the guidelines provided throughout this book.

This book is your best guide if you want to start your business in greenhouse gardening. It provides you with the basic information you'll need to start running a successful greenhouse garden. Provided in the book are all the details you need to become a professional gardener. If you want to get started now, you have chosen the right time to grab your copy; this will help you overcome any hurdles along the way and boost your confidence in greenhouse gardening.

Happy Gardening!

Part 2: Container Gardening

How You Can Create Your Own Small Garden and Grow Vegetables, Fruit, Flowers, and Herbs in Your Backyard, Indoors, or In Urban Areas

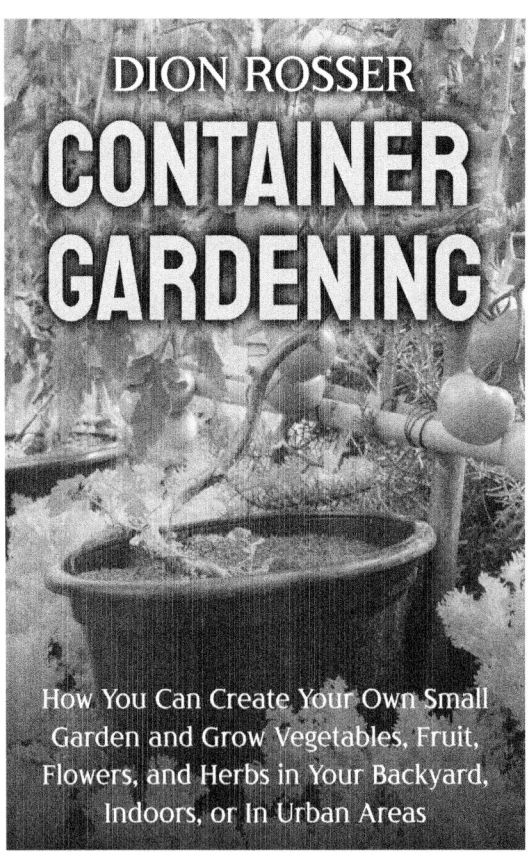

Introduction

If you do not have a big yard or lack outdoor space, indoor gardening is the way to go for any gardening enthusiast. Container gardening is one of the best options out there. This book will introduce you to what container gardening is and what it involves. It will also elaborate on how you can plan and prepare before getting started. As you read, you will learn more about different container options, ways to care for your container garden, how to maintain it, and what to do to avoid losing produce. It will also introduce you to the kinds of flowers, fruit, and vegetables you can start with.

Container gardening is one of the most popular methods of indoor gardening. This is because container gardens are easy to grow, control, and maintain. As the name suggests, these gardens involve using different kinds of containers, such as cans, pots, vessels, etc., for growing and housing plants. Standard plant pots can be used, but other kinds of containers can be great options to explore. The only thing you need to keep in mind is that they should have drainage holes that allow excess water to flow out. If you cannot get pots with drainage holes, opt for a larger pot and fill one-third with medium-sized gravel before adding the soil. This will ensure the roots have access to water but are not sitting in waterlogged soil.

With container gardening, you can utilize any space you have. Balconies, courtyards, even flat rooftops can work. You can also place pots around your house in spots where they have access to sunlight or other artificial light sources. Everything from fruits and vegetables to flowers can be grown in a container garden.

This book will also tell you how to prepare your containers before sowing seeds or transplanting a sapling into the containers. You will also get some great tips and tricks to understand better how you can improve your containers for better plant growth.

You will also be introduced to information on different containers and what you should place at the bottom of them. Many who are new to container gardening make the common mistake of choosing the wrong filler. With our help, you will learn what to do and how to ensure your soil drains well. You will also come across the necessary information you need to care for the containers and learn about growing flowers, fruit, vegetables, herbs, and the best practices to ensure better growth. Most people who start off with container gardening understandably make many mistakes. In this guide, we will be highlighting some common mistakes people make and tips on how you can overcome them.

If you want to master container gardening, you have come to the right place. With this book as your guide, all the information you need to start will be in your hands!

Chapter 1: What Is Container Gardening?

So, what is container gardening really? This is the question that will be explored in this chapter. We will explain what a container is (pot/barrel/bucket/etc.) and what it is not (raised garden beds). You will also get a clear idea of whom container gardening is for, with added details about living situations (limited space/budget/mobility or urban areas). A brief listing of what types of plants can be grown in a container garden will be covered in further detail later.

Put simply: container gardening involves the practice of growing plants in containers. It could be anything from a bush to a small tree. These containers can be as small as yogurt cups for small flowers or as big as a full-sized outdoor pot, which can house a tree. Container gardening has become especially popular in recent years as people move from spacious suburban homes to smaller, high-rise apartments. Regardless of where you live, it is something you should try your hand at. It is also a great option for those with a limited budget and who cannot afford all the equipment required for a large traditional garden.

A container garden will allow you to create a simple yet stylish garden space with low or high maintenance, depending on what you want. The best thing about it is that you have complete control over the design and layout. Containers can be set on the ground or shelves and tables, making it a feasible gardening option for those who have back issues, disabilities, or struggle to bend down comfortably while gardening. It makes gardening much less tedious and easier to manage. An added benefit is that container gardens are not as prone to weeds as outdoor gardens. Anyone can create a beautiful planting scheme with just a little work and a whole lot of creativity. It fits in well with a hardscape area, too.

Container gardening can add versatility to any garden, large or small. Plants are an excellent way to add color to your home and garden. These container plants can be placed on the ground in gardens, put on pedestals, mounted on windowsills, or hung on your porch. You can put them along the front walkway or driveway. Consider using container gardening to add some natural color to your patio or deck.

Large single containers can be used for outdoor decorating or as a focal point in the corner of a room. Small and large pots can also be combined on your patio, stairwell, or anywhere else in your garden. Hanging baskets and window boxes are an excellent way to enhance the appearance of your balcony or window spaces.

Growing a single species in containers is a stunning way to create garden highlights. This could be some ornamental grass or rosemary. Planting a variety of plants and experimenting with different combinations is another way to enjoy container gardening. In this instance, plants with attractive foliage and blossoms are ideal.

Including thrillers, fillers, and spillers is a simple approach to choose a combination for container gardens. First, add a thriller, which is the plant that will serve as the combination's focal point. This could be a colorful plant like coleus. Then, add the filler, which is typically a plant with smaller leaves or flowers that fills in the arrangement and adds color. Plants such as ornamental peppers, verbenas, and salvias are good filler options. You can also try foliage plants like licorice or parsley. For the spiller, add plants that grow to the point where they spill over the edge of the container. Plants like bacopa, ornamental sweet potatoes, and creeping zinnias can be used. This is the last element of the combination. Purple fountain grass, for example, will add height to these combinations. Growing vines on a trellis is another strategy to add height. If you have a large container, like twenty inches in diameter, you may need about five plants to fill it with a beautiful combination.

Container Sizes

It is important to note that growing plants in small containers is more difficult than growing plants in large containers. The main reason for this is that larger containers can retain more soil, keeping it moist for a longer time and allowing it to withstand rapid temperature changes. If you use small hanging baskets, you will find that they dry out quickly, and you may need to water them twice a day to keep them from dying, especially during summer.

It is also vital to think about the plants you would like to cultivate in the containers. A variety of factors determines the container's width and depth. A key determinant is the shape and size of the plant's root system that you want to cultivate. It also depends on whether the plant is a shrub, an annual, or a perennial and how rapidly the roots grow. When a plant is root-bound, it fills every inch of the soil it grows in, causing it to dry up quickly, stunting its growth. For mixed planting, choose a large container that will sufficiently accommodate each plant's root system. It is also recommended that you use a light-colored container to keep the soil cooler, while dark containers become heated quicker and retain heat longer.

The weight and size of the containers will be determined by the amount of space available in your home or garden, the surface on which they will be placed, and whether or not they will be relocated later on. Check how much weight the container can support if you are hanging it or putting it on a rack. A large, heavy container will suffice if you do not intend to relocate the containers at any point. However, if you intend to move them, they should be lighter and smaller so that you can easily relocate them when needed.

Container Drainage

Drainage holes should be present in whatever container you choose. The soil will become waterlogged, and your plants will die if the container does not have proper drainage. The container's holes must be large enough to allow excess water to drain. If you buy a container that doesn't have any holes, you can easily drill them yourself. Containers without holes should only be used as cachepots or as cover to conceal a plain pot. A cachepot helps manage large plants or heavy pots. You can get some decorative cachepots to conceal holes in ordinary nursery pots.

Containers such as hanging baskets, window boxes, self-watering containers, and double-walled containers are also available these days. These are good options for growing smaller plants that require frequent watering.

Container Materials

Each container material has its advantages and disadvantages.

Terracotta or clay containers are easily broken and damaged from thawing and freezing. They are an attractive choice, but these drawbacks must be considered. People in northern areas must store clay containers in a frost-free location to avoid cracking. These are also not suitable for shrubs or hardy perennials that you intend to keep outside all year.

Cast concrete containers are a great long-term option that come in various styles and sizes. You can also make them yourself, allowing your creativity to guide you. These containers can be left outside in any weather. If the container is made of plain concrete, it will be heavy and difficult to lift and move. In this case, they are better suited to plants that will be grown in the same location throughout the year. Concrete and fiberglass or concrete and vermiculite blends are much lighter blends. If you want a lightweight pot with a concrete aesthetic, hypertufa is a great choice.

Fiberglass and plastic planters or pots, which are available in various shapes and sizes, are inexpensive and lightweight options. Choose containers that are both sturdy and flexible. The stiff, thin ones will become brittle with age or when exposed to very cold weather.

Although polyurethane foam containers are about 90 percent lighter than clay or concrete containers, they have a similar appearance. This substance resists chipping and cracking. Polyurethane foam containers are especially suitable for plants that will be kept outdoors all year since they keep the roots insulated from cold or hot temperatures.

Wood planters are attractive and blend in well with your garden's natural elements. They also protect the plants from extreme temperature changes. If you have access to wood, you can even try creating them yourself. Woods that are resistant to rot, such as locust or cedar, should be used. Pine can also be used, but it must be preservative-treated. Plants are poisoned by creosote, so it should be avoided. Look for molded wood fiber pots, which are both inexpensive and sturdy.

Metal planters are durable and attractive, but they can conduct heat, exposing your plants to rapid temperature changes. Metal containers can be used to cover regular pots for plants that will be grown indoors. They are not suitable for use in an outdoor garden.

Container Preparation

Containers are often heavy, and once filled with soil, they become even heavier. As a result, consider where you want to put your container before filling it with soil and begin planting. If you cannot water them during the day, find a location where the plant will receive morning sunlight but will be sufficiently shaded when the sun reaches its peak during the day. Even if you wish to grow plants that require full sun, you must make sure they are not overheated. They will require less water if they are shaded in the afternoon than if they are under direct sunlight.

For your container garden, you should use pots with drainage holes. Before adding your potting mix, you do not have to fill these holes with gravel or pot shards. Pot shards can clog drainage holes, and plugging them will not enhance drainage. Before pouring the potting mix into the pot, line the base with newspaper or paper towels to keep the soil from washing down through the holes. If the container is deep, cover the bottom half of the pot with gravel or Styrofoam before adding the potting mix. This will reduce the amount of potting mix you will need, but you'll still need to ensure there is enough soil for the plant you are cultivating and its root system.

Plain garden soil is usually too dense for container gardening. If your container is approximately the size of a gallon, you can use a houseplant soil mix. Use a coarser, more soilless planting mixture if your container is significantly larger. This will restore the balance of air and water.

Before planting, the soil should be hydrated. Before filling the pot, water the soil or water the soil in the pot a few times before planting anything. After each watering, move the soil to ensure that it is evenly moistened. After you have sufficiently moistened the soil, you can begin planting.

For a mixed container, you can plant densely and ignore any spacing requirements. The plants will have to be pruned once you have planted and grown them. If you grow shrubs or trees, the circling roots must be trimmed off. The root ball should be covered to the same level as it was when being grown at the nursery. The soil mixture should be gently firmed down and then thoroughly watered. Pots should not be filled to the brim with soil. Leave space for watering.

Selecting Plants for Your Containers

Plants, herbs, flowers, shrubs, vegetables, and small trees can all be grown in containers. Compact and dwarf cultivars are best for a small pot. Plants should be chosen with consideration for the amount of sunlight and the climate. Consider how much shade the plant will receive. Containers containing fragrant plants should be protected from strong winds or breezes.

To generate an aesthetic appearance, get creative and blend trailing plants, flowers, and edibles. If you are not searching for a long-term option, container gardening can help you grow plants for years or even just a season. Remember that the roots are exposed to changing temperatures for permanent containers, making the plants less resistant. These plants must be relocated or supplied with additional winter protection from extreme winter temperatures. Since these pots may need to be moved, choose their weight carefully.

Vegetables

Single containers can be used to cultivate vegetables. A large pot or a half-barrel could be used. You can grow a tomato plant or some small vegetables like cabbage in a larger container. Bush or miniature varieties of some large plants, such as pumpkins or tomatoes, are suited for container gardening. You might even create a theme garden and make it a fun activity. Plants like chives, lettuces, and tomatoes can be used to make a salad garden. You may also grow the essential ingredients for pizza, such as tomatoes, peppers, and basil, in a "pizza garden."

Annuals

Plant annuals like marigolds or geraniums in your containers to keep them looking attractive all summer. You can choose plants that will bloom longer or have beautiful foliage by looking through a seed or garden catalog. Visit your local garden center to see what they have to offer; the staff should be able to advise you on what would work best for you, and you can test out different plants. If you have large containers, consider growing dwarf dahlias or dwarf cannas.

Perennials and Shrubs

Containers can be used to grow shrubs and perennials that will continue to grow throughout the years. Daylilies, hostas, and a variety of other perennials can easily be cultivated in container gardens. Lavender, ferns, sedges, and sedums are more options. Growing ornamental grass in containers is also a great idea.

Container Gardening vs. Raised Bed Gardening

Container gardening differs from the building of a raised garden bed. Many novice gardeners mix up container and raised bed gardening. Although you may normally plant directly in your backyard, the soil may not be adequate in some cases. Consider container gardening or a raised bed for your plants in these situations.

So, what exactly is the distinction between the two? A raised bed sits directly on the ground and raises the soil level by approximately two feet. In a container garden, enclosed pots that are not attached to the ground and are movable are used. Although raised beds are often larger than typical containers, some people use pots that may accommodate as much soil as a raised garden bed.

There are a few factors to consider when deciding between the two. You can choose the best type of gardening for your plants after weighing the benefits and disadvantages.

One of the most distinct differences is that potting containers have a bottom, whereas raised beds do not. A raised bed might sometimes just be piled soil and amendments with no sides. These are constructed directly on the soil without the need for any barriers and offer numerous benefits.

Advantages of raised beds:

- The drainage is better, and this helps to prevent root rot
- It allows for better entry of beneficial microbes through the garden
- The risk of fungal disease is significantly reduced
- Earthworms can enter and aerate the soil

Your plant will be grown in a suitable pot filled with potting soil or a decent compost mix in a container garden. The pot entirely encloses the soil and roots. While they are aesthetically part of the garden, they are independent and can be relocated to any position if the conditions are suitable for the plant.

Advantages of container gardening:

- It protects against pest infestation
- It reduces the risk of bacterial disease
- It is easier to move plants away from scorching sunlight when required
- It is convenient to relocate the plants during the winter

If you are unsure what sort of garden to go with, consider your available space. You must make the most of the space you have if you want to cultivate additional plants. Since the smallest raised bed will be around 4 x 4 feet, raised beds will demand additional space. If you have a proper pot, container gardening allows you to grow your plants almost anywhere. Container gardening is a great way to make the most of a limited patio or yard space.

Another important factor to consider is the plant you want to grow. Some plants thrive on raised beds, while others flourish in containers. Plants with deep roots will thrive in a raised bed; however, their growth would be restricted in a pot. The size of the plant also influences whether it is better to grow it in a container or not. Some plants have shallow roots, which make them ideal for container gardening, but if their top growth is large, the pot may not sustain them.

Most expert gardeners believe that a heavy plant with its support planted in a container can be too top-heavy and will frequently topple over. This can damage the plant, the pot, and anything else in the vicinity. If you leave the pot outside, a strong gust of wind could knock it over at any time. It is considerably easier to add support and cultivate top-heavy plants in a raised bed. If you must cultivate these plants in a pot, it must have a volume of at least five gallons.

Chapter 2: Having a Green Thumb

Have you ever visited a friend and been blown away by their beautiful garden? Does it inspire you to want to start your own garden, but you do not know how? Have you managed to destroy several beautiful plants you bought from the nursery? Don't despair; there is still hope. While some people are naturally good at cultivating plants, others must develop the skill. You don't have to be born with a green thumb; we will show you how to develop one!

Gardening is a beautiful, fun activity for everyone, and it is beneficial to both your physical and mental health. So, even if you are a gardening novice, apply these tips from experienced gardeners to successfully start growing plants. It is not rocket science, and it isn't something to be worried about. Even if you destroy a few plants along the way, you will be able to establish a beautiful garden that everyone will envy in no time.

Don't Take on More Than You Can Handle

Start small if you are a beginner. When you're just starting out, do not try to grow an entire garden or work with difficult plants. If you take on too much at once, you are more likely to fail and give up. The best strategy is to take things slowly. Begin with a few plants, or maybe just one, and work your way up from there. Learn as you go and learn what works for you and what does not. Soon, you will be able to grow a whole garden of healthy, lovely plants.

Figure Out What You Can Grow

Many individuals are unaware of the importance of planning a garden. First, you must understand the kind of plants that are appropriate for your climate and soil. This will help to determine what plants will survive and flourish and what ones will not. You may easily find this information online or in gardening guides for your particular region. Instead of trying to grow something that is more likely to die in an environment like this, acquire seeds or plants that you know would thrive in that climate. For instance, plants that cannot withstand high heat should not be grown in a tropical climate, and, similarly, plants that require a lot of sunlight should not be grown in a place that barely gets any exposure to sunlight during the day.

Pick the Plants You Want to Grow

Now that you know what will grow well in your region, you must select the plants you prefer among those that are available. Are you seeking a productive kitchen garden where you grow herbs and vegetables? Are you seeking to beautify your environment with colorful floral plants? What kinds of plants do you wish to experiment with? If you want to grow vegetables, lettuce and tomatoes are the best choices to start with. These are simple plants that most beginners can grow, and you can obtain a high yield for your efforts. Thus, choose the plants you want to grow and get seeds or plants from a nursery. Look up instructions for growing the plants you chose and follow through until you see your efforts pay off. Start with the basics. Avoid trying to grow exotic plants that you cannot even spell properly. Look at what your neighbor is growing and ask them what is easy to start with. Plant something that will easily thrive in your soil.

Get Some Gear

You do not need to spend a lot of money or buy a complete toolbox. However, you will need to invest in some basic gardening equipment to help you grow your plants successfully. Get a full-sized shovel if you have an outdoor lawn or garden. If you only have containers, a small hand trowel will suffice. A bypass is required for mild pruning and deadheading. A garden knife is required for splitting plants and digging out weeds. Also, get some gardening gloves to protect your hands while working in the dirt.

Learn How to Water

Many people think watering is a simple task and that you just need to drench your plants every day to keep them healthy. The truth is: there is a fine line between too little and too much water. Each plant needs to be watered differently. While some plants need to be watered every day, others may only need to be watered weekly. Overwatering or under-watering will kill your plants or increase the possibility of root rot and mold. You need to determine how much to water the plants you pick and how often they need watering.

Explore the Seasons

Try growing plants in every season. Do not give up when the seeds you planted in summer don't grow. You can try winter plants, which may grow just fine for you. Each season allows you to explore different varieties of plants, and you can try a few different ones every year as you enjoy gardening more. Begin with simple, seasonal herbs or vegetables that you can serve with your meals. For instance, some great options for cold weather plants include kale, beets, and spinach. These will thrive in the winter months, and you can even grow them in your greenhouse if the weather is hot where you live.

Pick the Right Spots

Plants will grow well if they are placed in an environment that they will thrive in. An indoor plant that needs very little light will not do well under direct sunlight on your lawn for seven hours a day. Similarly, a plant that needs six–seven hours of sunlight will not grow well if you place it indoors, where it only gets two hours of artificial light a day. Look up the requirements of the plant you are growing and place it under the appropriate conditions.

Fix Your Soil

Digging a hole in the ground and putting some seeds in it is not enough. Most people do not have access to the ideal soil for their plants to grow in. However, this is not a dealbreaker for your garden since you can amend the soil. First, you need to choose plants that grow well in the type of soil in your backyard. If you want to grow plants that need other soil types, buy a few bags of that soil. Otherwise, use materials like compost or peat moss to improve your soil. If you are growing plants in containers, you need to get a high-quality potting mix labeled suitable for pots or raised beds.

Make a List Before Buying Plants

Make a list before you go to a nursery or anywhere else to buy new plants. Learn more about the plants you wish to grow and are capable of caring for. This will help you avoid confusion or panic when shopping for plants. To help you choose, you might check through plant catalogs or look up information online. Then make a list of the plants, the number and size of the containers you will need, and any other requirements for your garden. If you already have pots, you need to choose plants that are suited for them. Someone at the nursery will usually be capable and willing to help you with this.

Pick the Right Neighbors for Your Plants

Not all plants grow well together. Whether you are growing a combination of plants in the same pot or planning to grow them near each other, you need to figure out the best neighbors. The plants you grow in the same pot should require the same kind of soil, light, and moisture. You cannot grow a plant that needs a lot of water with a plant that only needs watering once a week. A plant that needs full sun will not grow well with a plant that needs more shade. Check the requirements of each plant before placing them together.

Fertilize

Just like our bodies need proper nutrition, so do plants. Occasionally providing them with a bit of nutritional boost will do wonders for their growth. Fertilizing the plant will help ensure good growth. These days you have access to slow-releasing fertilizers that make it easier for beginners who do not know much about gardening. Get some low-nitrogen, slow-releasing fertilizer and add it during planting. This will take care of the nutrition needs of your plant for a few seasons. Don't be concerned about the quantity because there is usually never too little or too much. If you cannot find a slow-release fertilizer, consider applying a liquid fertilizer every two weeks or so. Diluted compost tea, seaweed extract, or fish emulsion are the best options. If you are growing nightshade vegetables, such as potatoes, tomatoes, and eggplants, you can use a tomato feed, which can be purchased online or at any garden center.

Weed

Weeding is another crucial aspect of gardening that should not be overlooked. Weeding regularly is just as essential as watering on time. Examine your pots to determine if any noxious weeds have sprouted. Weeds will hinder the growth of your plants and can even destroy healthy ones. Dig out any stray sprouts from the pots every few days.

Dust off the Plants

Whether you grow your plants indoors or outdoors, dust them off occasionally. Some plants tend to catch a lot of dust and need to be regularly wiped off. Too much dust can clog the pores of your plants and prevent them from getting adequate light, too. The dust usually washes off when you water them down. However, also try using a damp cloth to wipe the leaves in between watering sessions.

Most importantly, keep trying. The main difference between someone with a green thumb and someone without it is that the former keeps trying while the latter gives up in the face of obstacles or failure. You can develop a green thumb if you put in a bit of effort and time. Some plants will die along the way, but that is all right. The experience will teach you what you should and should not be doing the next time. Keep at it, and you will be rewarded with the literal fruit of your efforts in due time. Grow some beautiful flowers or grow your own produce. Dig in and start growing.

Chapter 3: What's in a Container?

This chapter will dive specifically into container basics. It will discuss the different containers you can use when planting and their key features (such as self-watering pots and how metal containers make for hotter, dryer growing conditions). It will also list some unconventional containers like old tires, mason jars, DIY wooden containers, etc.

Types of Gardening Containers

Raised Container Garden

A sturdy wood container can retain a lot of water. If you use an old crate or a twig-built container, it must be lined with a water-resistant material before being filled with soil. Burlap can be used for a rustic aesthetic effect, but it must be lined with plastic to last the season. Do not forget to drill a few drainage holes in the bottom of the plastic lining.

Concrete Container Garden

https://pixabay.com/photos/boxwood-buxus-book-green-370547/

Concrete containers are a heavy option that add character to your garden. They have traditional patterns and angular lines. The material allows for good insulation to the soil and moderates soil temperature as well as moisture loss. The heavy weight means you should only use them in places where you will not have to move the containers again.

Metal Container Garden

https://pixabay.com/photos/hyacinths-container-onions-basket-1286716/

If you want a more modern, slicker feel for your garden, use metal containers. Be careful about choosing the plants you will place in them. Metal containers get hot fast and quickly dry out the soil, too. You can use them for plants that can withstand drought and heat. The containers should be kept near a source of water so you can water as often as required. For an urban look, pair these containers with pebble mulch.

Terra-cotta Pot Container Garden

Terracotta or clay pots are available in all kinds of shapes, sizes, and styles. If the pots are unglazed, they are porous, making the soil dry out quickly. These pots are suitable for shady areas. You can grow lavender and similar Mediterranean herbs in unglazed terracotta containers without issue. For a sunny spot, use glazed terracotta pots. Note that the pots made in warmer areas will not withstand a long freezing winter and are liable to chip or flake.

Stone Pot Container Garden

https://pixabay.com/photos/palm-stone-pot-plant-vase-wall-3373652/

For a graceful, old-school style in your garden, choose stone pots. Stone pots look better as they age and tend to acquire a moss coating that adds a wistful feel to your garden. Stone is a great material for places where the winters are frost-prone, and it insulates the soil, preventing heat and moisture loss. Since stone is a heavy material, the pots should be placed before they are filled with soil or any planting is done. You may also note that these pots are expensive, but they last forever and are worth the investment.

Hypertufa Container Garden

Handmade hypertufa is an easy way to get the look of stone containers in your garden. These pots are much lighter than stone or concrete and can easily be made by mixing quick-setting concrete with perlite and peat moss. These containers are quite porous and ideal for succulents and alpine plants since they need good drainage.

Grow Bag Container Garden

Grow bags are the most convenient way to grow plants in any location. They are made of polypropylene blends that are lightweight and flexible. Plant roots can breathe freely in them, and they protect against overwatering. Grow bags also keep heat from accumulating in the soil. These factors promote the growth of a healthy root system, which in turn boosts plant growth. Bags should be emptied and folded away to store in colder climates.

Self-watering Plastic Pot Container Garden

Self-watering containers allow you to go easy on the watering schedule. They have a built-in water reservoir, which keeps your soil moist for longer. If you choose baskets, make sure the hanging hardware will support the heavy weight that water will add to the pots. They should also have drainage holes, or the soil will get waterlogged when exposed to rainy weather.

Resin Planter Garden

You can use faux stone containers that are mixed with resins, fiberglass, and stone aggregates. This container will look like a regular stone planter but is much lighter. It is a great option for use on a staircase or deck where heavy pots made of stone may cause damage. Moss can grow on these containers, but they do not age the same way as real stone pots. They are also a great option to protect your plants from frost.

Plastic Container Garden

https://pixabay.com/photos/plants-flowerpot-plastic-color-2810508/

Plastic containers come in all sorts of colors and designs. These can help you jazz up your garden or home more than the traditional container options. You can get plastic containers shaped like traditional clay pots as well as those that look like tubs. Plastic containers are durable, lightweight, and frost-proof. The material is not porous, and this allows the soil to remain moist for longer, which, in turn, means you do not have to water as frequently as you would otherwise have to. If you expose dark-colored plastic containers to too much direct sunlight, they will heat the soil, and the pots can become brittle after a while.

Unconventional Container Garden Ideas

Bucket Garden

https://pixabay.com/photos/bucket-diy-plant-pot-plant-cress-2804814/

Buckets are one of the cheapest and easiest options to start your own container garden. You can use any kind of bucket you already have at home and start gardening with it. For instance, you might have some empty buckets left over from painting your house. Just clean them out with hot water to sterilize them. Then make some holes at the bottom for drainage. Layer the bottom of the bucket with gravel (up to an inch). Then fill them with potting soil and start planting. Buckets are a good container option for growing vegetables such as potatoes, tomatoes, and garlic. For vegetables that grow underground, you need slightly larger buckets with more depth to give the vegetables enough room to grow. Buckets are convenient because they may be carried and placed anywhere. So, if you are planting anything that requires a lot of sunlight, move your bucket to a sunny location. If you subsequently replace the plant but use the same bucket and require more shade, you may easily move the bucket to a more suitable location.

Compost Bag Garden

Compost bags can also be used to grow plants if you do not have buckets handy. If you buy compost in bulk, you save money by using compost bags that you can directly plant in. Just make sure you shake the bag so that the compost is loose. Don't plant in compact compost. Now cut slots in the compost bag. The number of slots will depend on what kind of plant you want to grow. Make three cuts if you want to grow tomatoes, for example. Once the cuts are made, you can sow your seeds or plant some seedlings into the slot. Water them appropriately and place them in the right location so that the plant gets as much sun as it needs. Seedlings can be planted directly into the slots, but you can also use growth rings. Growth rings make it easier for you to water the plants, which is also beneficial for the plant. Compost bags are not a good option for growing plants such as beets or potatoes since their soil is not very thick.

Old Tire Garden

https://pixabay.com/photos/tire-old-car-flower-garden-tires-5261233/

168

Many people use old tires to grow plants, and it is something you should try as well; however, there are some things to consider when doing this. Once old tires start breaking down, they will add toxins to the soil in them. If you are growing vegetables, you will be exposed to these toxins upon consumption. This problem does not occur initially and is not a problem if you are only growing ornamental plants.

If you plan on leaving your tires out in the sun, avoid using black tires. They absorb a lot of heat, which causes the soil to dry up. Tires are heavy, so keep them in a location where you will not have to move them again. Tires should be placed on land because they do not have a bottom. You can make your tires more appealing and add a fun element to your container garden by painting them in different colors. Almost anything can be grown in tires, so experiment with different plants based on tire size and growing space requirements.

Plastic Bottle Garden

Many people reuse plastic bottles to grow plants. You may have even have done this yourself in a science class at school. Thus, the next time you buy a bottle of water or a soda, do not throw the bottle out. The same concern from using old tires is applicable here; over time, plastic can release toxins into the soil. There are seven kinds of plastic bottles that are sold in the market. The ones that are safe for use include PET, HDPE, LDPE, and PP plastics.

Plastic bottles are a great option for growing your own salad, though bigger veggies can only be grown in big bottles. Microgreens easily grow in normal plastic bottles. Use coconut coir instead of potting soil for microgreens. Other plants will necessitate the use of potting soil mix. To make the bottles look nice, paint the outsides in different colors or designs. Reusing plastic bottles is an environmentally friendly choice that helps limit the amount of plastic garbage that ends up in the ocean or underground.

One-pot Garden

https://pixabay.com/photos/flower-flower-pots-plants-508204/

A one-pot garden is a good option for those who do not have much space to work with. A single pot can be used for planting many seeds or seedlings. They are especially great for growing an herb garden. You just need a pot, seeds, and potting soil. Other than herbs, you can also try growing strawberries in this kind of pot. Hang the pot up or place it in an empty corner. If you want to grow an herb garden, you can use the herbs you buy at the grocery store instead of buying seeds, and these will grow out. Note that your plants will grow better if you use proper potting mix instead of the usual garden soil. You can also help the herbs grow a small root system in a plastic bottle filled with water before placing them in the pot. Plants such as mint, parsley, basil, and rosemary are great options for one-pots.

PVC Pipe Garden

Old PVC pipes can be used for growing plants, too. They are primarily used for growing salad greens and herbs. Make some holes in the pipe and start using them as pots. Potting mix can be added along the length of the pipe before sowing seeds into the holes. Spinach, kale, watercress, arugula, basil, mint, and lettuce grow well in PVC pipes. If you want to build a vertical vegetable garden, PVC pipes are your best bet. Vertical gardens are an ideal solution to having a limited area to work with and substantially increasing your gardening production. Since most pipes come in white, you can choose to paint them in different colors if you want your garden to look more vibrant. When you notice your PVC pipes start to break down, throw them out since they release toxins into the soil, too. You can also consider using PVC pipes for growing a hydroponic garden. PVC pipes can be installed inside your home, outside in the garden, or even inside a greenhouse. If you grow indoors, use some grow lights to promote better growth.

Old Tree Garden

If you have any old tree stumps lying around or can get some for free, you can use them as a container for your garden. You can carve out the middle of the tree to insert soil and then fill it with potting soil and start planting. These old tree stumps look lovely in their natural condition and will add charm to your home or garden. Water the plants as needed, but avoid overwatering, harming the plant, and destroying the stump.

Mason Jar Garden

https://pixabay.com/photos/greenforest-glass-plant-home-decor-1626818/

It is incredible when you think about all the different ways that mason jars and glass jars can be used. For now, consider using them for growing an herb garden. Clean out a few of your old mason jars—or get some new ones if you want since they are inexpensive—and layer them with pebbles and potting mix, and then plant your seeds or seedlings. Now all you need to do is water them on time, and you can easily grow your own herbs. Just place these jars along a windowsill in your kitchen or wherever you want to give them the sunlight and air they need. Regularly check the soil to see if it is dry and needs watering or moist and can wait. Overwatering can kill the herbs. While harvesting, just makes small cuttings or pick out only how much you need. Do it so that the plant is not hurt and continues to give you produce.

Barrel Garden

Barrels are also a fun way to grow plants in containers. They have a lot of depth and are a good option for underground vegetables such as potatoes or any plant that needs more space for the root system. You can grow a lovely salad garden in barrels as well. Place these out in the garden or even on your patio.

As you can see, containers come in a wide range of shapes, sizes, and styles, allowing you to be quite creative with your container garden. Container gardening is ideal when you do not have much land to work with or only want to cultivate a few plants.

Chapter 4: How to Prep Your Pot

Now that you know about the different types of pots, you should know what goes into them (before the plant does). The importance of this step is to ensure the plants can properly thrive in the container. You will need to know about creating drainage holes, inserting pebbles or rocks for drainage under the soil, what type of soil is best for each plant, how to lighten a heavy pot, and if using pot liners is a good idea. This chapter also highlights the positive outcomes of each step and the potential negative outcomes of skipping them.

We will look at how you can ready your containers before you plant seeds. You cannot dump some soil or potting mix in the container and just have the plant grow. The following are some things to remember when preparing your plants:

- Ensure your container or pot is filled with the right potting mixture. Also, ensure that the mix is right.

- Do not put Styrofoam, rocks, broken pieces of pots, paper, or other material at the bottom of the container. This is not going to improve the drainage of the soil. If you do this, the opposite is going to happen.

- Never fill the container with any soil you have removed from the beds in your garden; this material is very dense for your pot.

Once you fill the container with soil, you need to complete the following steps before your container is ready for planting:

- Water the soil in the pot thoroughly. You can use a slow stream of water based on how dry your potting soil is. You may need to water the soil a few times to ensure it is wet.

- It is good to use lukewarm water as it works better for the soil than cold water. The former can saturate the soil. You can leave the hose under the sun for a bit and then let the water run through the hose. The water will be slightly warm, and this is good for your potting mix.

- Do not only dampen your soil; this is not going to moisten the soil enough. It is essential to water the soil enough for the roots to grow well in the soil.

- It is also crucial to water the plants carefully. Do not squirt the water onto the soil, which makes a mess and does not moisten the soil. The odds are that you may lose a lot of potting soil when you do this.

When your soil is moist and saturated, follow the steps given below:

- Do not sow the seeds or move the plants into the pot immediately since the soil is damp.

- Let the containers drain the water and wait for some time. Create a well-drained and moist environment in the container to plant.

You may be wondering if this will work for all containers, regardless of their size or material of construction. Yes, it does. If you use ceramic containers, this will also work. Even if you have a foam garden or a plastic jar, you can use this method.

Fill the pots with soil from your garden area and soak the material if you want to reduce waste. You can ensure that the water draining from the containers is used to water the soil in this manner.

When your pots are filled with well-drained, moist potting soil, you can set up the containers and sow the seeds. It is that easy! Congratulations, you now know how to prepare your containers and set up the garden by yourself. This garden can have flowers, vegetables, fruit, and other miniature herbs and shrubs. You are all set to prepare your plants.

The following are the steps to follow:

Prepare Your Containers

You cannot start planting until your pots are filled with suitable soil. Ensure the pots are prepared well and drain properly. You also need to protect them from different elements.

Check for Drain Holes

Most pots, especially ceramic pots, have drain holes to keep excess water from rotting the roots. Most non-traditional and plastic containers lack the necessary drainage holes. If your pot lacks adequate holes, drill them yourself.

If the pot did not come with the necessary holes, bore some holes in the container with a half-inch drill bit. Check that they are evenly spaced. Make sure you use the proper drill or equipment to make holes in the containers, as different materials may require different tools.

Stop the Plants from Rotting

If you want your plants to grow and be healthy, let the water drain well. Use a layer of gravel or a fine mesh to ensure the soil can drain the water well. These materials ensure the water drains through the soil.

Do Not Add Too Much Soil

If you add too much soil to the container or pot, it will be too heavy for you to move, especially after you water it. If you want to reduce the container's weight, fill the bottom with the right soil or potting mix, and do not go overboard.

Choose the Right Soil

We have been talking a lot about drainage and watering; however, the most important thing to consider is the soil. It is one of the most important factors if you want your garden to succeed. Some soil mixes come with the right potting mixture, formulated with the right proportions of every component.

The mixes labeled as topsoil or garden soil cannot be used since they are dense. They can't be used in containers since the water will not drain, causing the roots to dry out. Potting mixes are beneficial to your plants because they are light and airy and aid in water retention.

You need to prepare your pots the right way so that your plants do not die. It is only when you master this that you can have a thriving garden. Your plants are not going to do well in a pot if the water does not drain. If the water stagnates or does not reach the roots, the roots may die. Your roots may also die or suffer in the stagnation. This only makes it harder for your plants to survive. Your plants will turn yellow, wilt, and die. Thus, protect your containers if you want your plants to survive and do well.

Chapter 5: Container Care 101

This chapter will discuss the crucial steps to maintain your container garden and care for the containers themselves. You will want to thoroughly learn about watering (how much, how often), fertilizing (compost, plant food, or premixed soil), pruning (how and why), and rotating for full sun coverage (if possible). In this section, there are additional tips and care instructions that gardeners can use throughout the growing season. We will also talk about replanting as an option if the plant has outgrown its original pot. Finally, there is a section at the end for winter care of plants and pots—for instance, it explains why pots will need to be brought inside (certain stone pots can break in freezing temperatures) or stored in a basement to keep the entire root from freezing.

Caring for Your Container Garden

Water Your Container Garden

Most gardeners enjoy the designing and planting aspects of gardening but neglect the maintenance part. If you want your container garden to thrive, you need to care for the plants properly. This will help you make the most of those vegetables, fruits, or flowers you planted with care. One of the essential parts of caring for a container garden is watering. Containers restrict the amount of space available to your plants, and the roots can only access the amount of water that the container can hold. If these plants are not irrigated regularly, it causes plant stress, and they are more prone to disease and pest infestations.

When your container garden is not watered regularly, it will affect the growth of the plants and reduce the vegetable or flower yield. When the weather is warm, the pots need more frequent watering. Check to see that at least twenty percent of the water exits the bottom when you water the pot. This will flush out any excess fertilizer salts from the soil. When the weather is cooler, watering need not be as frequent, but you must check to see that the soil is moist in between watering. Simply stick one finger into the soil and check if the soil is dry at the top. When the soil is dry, you have to water it. If it is moist, you can wait a day or two to water again.

Fertilize

Another challenge you will have while cultivating a container garden is determining whether or not the plants are receiving enough nutrition to thrive. As plants grow and mature, they consume the nutrients in the potting soil. When you water the plant, certain nutrients are lost as they are drained out. As a result, it is critical to fertilize the soil to replenish nutrients. Add some granular fertilizer to your container when you first plant in it. This will ensure that your seeds or seedlings have a healthy start. During the growing season, add a weekly dose of liquid fertilizer when watering the plants. Be sure to determine exactly how much you should be fertilizing, and do not add more than required. Different plants have different fertilizer requirements at times. This information is easily accessible online or on the back of the seed packet. You can also ask someone with more experience for advice.

Pest Management

You must check your containers several times per week to see if there is any evidence of pests or diseases. The signs will vary depending on what plant you are growing. You may notice some missing flower buds or nibbled blossoms. There might be pock-marked leaves or skeletonized foliage. You must identify the pest before you take steps to get rid of it. If you do not take the right course of action, you may end up harming the plant instead of protecting it. You can consult a pest ID guide to identify the type of pest affecting your garden and then use the most effective method to get rid of them without harming your plants.

Deadheading

Deadheading may sound a little weird, but it just means that the dead blooms are lopped off the plant. You may have noticed how the flowers on your plant just shrivel up at some point. When you get rid of these spent flowers, it is called deadheading. Flowers such as petunias can be easily pulled off from their stem. Some, like marigolds, will have to be pinched, while coneflowers need to be trimmed with scissors or pruners. The stem holding the bloom can be snipped off near the first few leaves on it. All of this is called deadheading.

Plants can grow to be too tall or large for their containers, making them look unattractive. In such instances, you may need to do some cutting back. Cutting back encourages more compact growth and the development of several flowers on a single stalk rather than multiple stems. The containers should also be turned around a bit from time to time. This will ensure that each part of the plant gets equal exposure to sunlight and not just one part. When certain parts of the plant struggle to reach the light, the plant begins to look straggly. When your container herbs are established, pinch the main stem back. New branches will grow from this part, and the plant will fill out. Cutting back helps herbs increase their production. When you see flowers grow, you can pinch these off, too. Once the plant grows full and large, many herbs can be cut to dry, freeze, or use. The general rule of thumb is to trim off any old stems, leaves, or growth. This will help keep your plants compact and encourage new growth.

Pruning is another important part of container maintenance. When you have large plants in your container garden, pruning is essential for plant care. It will help improve their shape and promote good health for the plant. Cut any damaged, dead, or diseased parts of the plant. Any excessive branch growth should also be removed. This kind of pruning will allow more sunlight to reach all plants and help achieve good airflow. While pruning a tree or shrub, branches should be cut back at different lengths. This will give the plant a natural appearance after pruning. You can cut just above any buds or at the branch unions.

When you groom your plant by thinning, it does not change the shape, but it still promotes flowering. This will involve the complete removal of a branch. It is also crucial to remove the whole branch from the main trunk or stem without leaving a stub. The plant will become infected as a result of such stubs. Some plants require pruning in the early spring, while others require pruning near the end of the winter. You can look up pruning instructions for the plant you are cultivating. Pruning should be avoided during the hottest times of the day. In general, the best time to prune deciduous plants is early spring. This gives the plant enough time to heal before the arrival of winter. For fast-growing plants, you can prune them any time during the season.

Replanting

Replanting is required at times when maintaining a container garden. It will keep your container plants looking their best through the seasons. When you see a plant die or wilt, for any reason, pull it out and sow another plant. You can even do this when a plant has passed its blooming season. Replanting can be done to change plants during a change in seasons as well. For instance, you can switch out your geraniums for spurge or African daisies. Try to keep your containers full of healthy plants through each season and replant accordingly.

Large trees, shrubs, or perennials may outgrow their pot or box at some point. This is when you need to repot them into a larger pot to allow proper growth. Repot in a container double the original size so that you do not have to do it again for a while. While replanting, the larger roots of the plant should be cut back to about one-third of their size. You need to check that the roots don't circle each other in a ball, either. If you find that is the case, loosen the roots before replanting in the larger pot. Use fertilizer and fresh potting soil at the time of replanting.

Winterize Your Container Plants

When you create a container garden outdoors, you will usually grow some annual species that get discarded around the end of fall and replace them with new plants in spring. You may also be growing perennial plants in your outdoor containers, and these can be kept alive through the cold winter months. While this is possible, it is not easy. Even if your plants are cold-hardy, you need to take a little extra care to protect them through the winter. While these cold-hardy species may survive through a harsh winter when grown in soil, it is not always the case in a container garden. Therefore, you need to ensure proper care when growing perennials or any plants through the winter.

Weather intensity can be correlated with the geographic zone you are in. These zones are enumerated, and different plant species will grow in each various zone. Generally, you must rate your perennial plant for about two hardy zones colder than its usual growing climate for it to survive through the winter. For instance, if you are in zone 5, you can expect a perennial rated for zone 3 to survive cold weather when grown in containers. Some plants can survive a light frost, but others can die when the harsh winter causes their cells to freeze. The hardiness of the plant will determine how it responds to the first frost of the season.

Some container plants will simply go dormant like other garden plants. However, if the temperature keeps dropping and gets too cold, the plant roots may die if not protected. You need to take steps to protect your potted perennial about a week or so before you expect the first frost to hit. The following steps will help keep your container plants safe and ensure they survive the cold winter healthily.

Equipment required is:

- Trowel or shovel
- Gravel
- Chicken wire
- Stakes
- Mulch, straw, or leaves for insulation

Instructions

1. *First, check your container to see if it will last through a cold winter.* If your container is very porous, it has a higher chance of cracking. Materials such as plastic are resilient and will tolerate freezing temperatures. Materials such as terracotta and other natural materials will absorb water quite readily, and when they freeze, the pot will expand and crack. The first step to harden your plant is to ensure that it is in a container made from any material that will withstand cold temperatures. If it's not, consider repotting the plant in something more suitable.

2. *Choose a shelter for your plants.* Find some spots on your lawn or in the garden to keep your plants sheltered through the winter. Dig a hole that is a bit deeper than your container's depth. Keep the width of the hole a little wider than the container to provide extra

room around its edges.

3. *Make a layer of gravel.* Once you have dug a hole, spread a layer of gravel in it. This will allow drainage in the spring when the pot thaws. The soil in containers usually defrosts quicker than the garden soil around the pot, making drainage an issue.

4. *Place the container into the hole.* After you layer with gravel, you can place your pot inside the hole. Now spread some garden soil on top of the buried pot. The rim of your container should ideally be slightly below the ground level surrounding the hole. This will allow you to cover with garden soil without any lumpy soil on the surface. You can mark this spot if you want, and this will help you locate your plant easily when spring comes around.

5. *Winterize the plant.* The buried plant should be winterized, just like any other plant that you grow in the ground. For instance, you can mulch over the buried container or spread leaves, or compost over that spot.

6. *Dig out the plant.* Once spring arrives, take the potted plant out from the hole. Once you notice the ground thawing and some new growth coming in, lift the pot out. This container plant can now be moved back to its usual spot in spring.

Sheltering Container Plants for Winter

Plants are not usually killed by the cold temperatures of winter. Plant stress could be caused by fast temperature fluctuations between summer heat and winter cold as it thaws and freezes. You can provide shelter and a higher chance of survival for your container plants by shielding them from temperature changes. This can be done in many ways:

- **Cluster the potted plants**: Take your potted plants and cluster them together in some sheltered spot in your garden or home, like against a wall. This will protect them from harsh winds that can cause the temperature to drop rapidly. It will also allow the cluster of pots to receive some heat from the house. Pick a spot that gets enough shade. While sunlight is important, keeping your perennial protected from the thaw/freeze cycle will help it survive the winter. The pots should be placed in a spot where they are not exposed to very dramatic temperature changes.

- **Give additional shelter**: After you cluster the potted plants in a sheltered location, provide some added shelter. This can be done by covering them with straw, a tarp, or other types of insulating materials. This additional layer of shelter will help control the temperature changes and reduce the chances of your perennials dying once it gets cold.

- **Build some insulated silos around your potted plants.** Many gardeners like building insulating silos around their containers. This is especially so in the case of delicate plants, such as potted roses. You can build an insulated silo with some chicken wire and stakes. Form a type of enclosure around the container plant and fill the silo with straw or loose leaves, keeping the plant cozy.

Moving Your Container Garden Indoors During Winter

One simple method to protect your perennials during winter is to move them indoors. This technique works best for tropical perennial plants that grow during winter. Thus, if you have some begonias, consider bringing them indoors before winter arrives. If you have planted some fruit trees in containers and grow them on your patio or deck during the summer, these can be moved indoors for winter as well. However, plants that need winter dieback and have a normal dormancy period should be kept outdoors through winter. Find a position that will give enough light to the other perennials when you transfer them indoors. Providing enough sunlight might be challenging during the winter because the sun is usually low in the sky, and the days are shorter. Keep an eye out for the areas that receive the most light and place the containers there. Another concern is that it can get quite dry indoors during winter, and perennials that require humidity may not do so well under this condition. Even in dry winter conditions indoors, purchasing a humidifier may help them survive.

Container Care

Now that you know the basics of caring for your container garden, let us talk about caring for the actual containers.

Once the blooming season ends, empty and clean any containers you will not use during the winter. This will keep them ready for planting during the spring.

Throw out any old potting mix, or they could become a home for pests and their larvae. Use some dish soap and water for washing out your pots. If you see any pest or disease in the soil or plant grown, the pot should be dipped in a mild water and bleach solution. Once you clean out the containers, dry them out in the sun.

In the winter, you can take some time to decorate your containers if you are not using them or if they appear a little worn. Put on a fresh coat of paint or touch up any chipped bits. When you paint your plant containers, remember to add a few coats of polyurethane to them, which will weatherproof them.

Tools for Container Gardening

If you want a healthy indoor garden, your work will need to go beyond just picking seeds and potting. You must continue to care for the plants until they are ready for the harvest season. While you do not need to spend all day tending to these plants, you do need to dedicate a little time to them. When a novice or layperson thinks of gardening, huge tools such as shovels, spades, and rakes come to mind. These are tools for gardening or farming outdoors. They are practical, and you can use them in your garden. However, you need some other simple tools to help ensure your container garden is a success.

Hand Fork

Growing plants indoors has one drawback: they do not have access to as many nutrients as plants grown outdoors. Therefore, the gardener must make an extra effort to provide the required nutrients to the indoor container plants regularly. This will ensure that the indoor plant remains healthy and thrives. Compost and fertilizer are important for plants, and they must be well distributed into the growing medium. For this very purpose, you need a hand fork at the ready. Most hand forks have three or more prongs. The prongs are used for navigating the soil so it can be aerated, and the nutrients can settle into the soil evenly. Hand forks are useful when planting or transplanting. In the case of very small plants, a table fork can easily be used. You just need to bend it as required and then use it as a garden hand fork.

Watering Can

Many people assume that watering cans are a one-size-fits-all tool; however, this is not true. A watering can that is efficient for your outdoor garden may not be suitable for your indoor garden. For watering containers, look for a smaller can. Get a watering can that is lightweight and has a long, thin neck. It will help you have more control over the amount of water you pour over the plant. Ensure that the can is easy to clean to prevent contamination.

Pruner

Purchase a standard set of pruners because they will be used frequently in the garden. They are great for trimming leaves, stems, and weeds because they're so precise and accurate. After each usage, this tool must be cleaned. If you leave the pruner dirty, it can cause disease or damage your plants. Use an alcohol wipe if you use the pruner on any diseased plants or even while cleaning in general. Any disease-carrying components on your tool will be removed as a result.

Transplanter

As you know, container gardens do not have as much space as outdoor gardens. Therefore, plants must be transferred from pot to pot as they grow. Transplanters are used to make this easy. If you have this tool, you will find it much easier to plant bulbs as well. This will make both tasks easier and faster.

Hand Rake

Hand rakes or cultivators are handy tools when preparing the soil at the beginning of the growing season. A hand rake will help you loosen up the soil and break it up. The process is much easier and faster with this tool, and most experienced gardeners recommend it. A hand rake usually has five claws attached to the tool's base with a wooden handle. The blend of steel and wood provides balance. It is effortless to use and makes a lot of difference for your container care.

Moisture Meter

Another tool that makes it easy to handle watering problems for your container garden is a moisture meter. It will help you resolve the issue of underwatering or overwatering. The meter will detect the level of water in the soil and determine when it needs water. It is easy to use since it has a color-coded gauge that helps you detect the moisture level. Another advantage is that this tool does not require batteries.

Grow Lights

Understanding the light requirements of any plant you grow is very important, especially in indoor gardens; you must provide the plants with adequate light. If your containers do not have access to enough natural sunlight, you need to use grow lights. These artificial light sources are the next best option for sunlight and ensure that your plants get as many hours of light as needed for growth. There are many different grow lights to choose from, and it will mostly depend on your budget and what your plants need. Buy a few grow lights for containers you place in corners that barely see any light.

Wi-Fi Plant Sensor

A new age gardening tool to consider is a Wi-Fi plant sensor. This tool is mobile app-enabled and helps beginners garden like professionals. You do not have to break a sweat or pay for gardening lessons. The built-in sensors in the tool will help monitor the moisture levels and temperature of the soil and the amount of light the plant is receiving. The device is small and looks like a golf club. It uses a web or mobile app to help the gardener track the plants. You can easily tell when your container needs to be watered or is not getting enough light when you use this tool.

Trowel

Trowels are a small hand-held tool that you will use to dig, apply, smooth, or move material in your container. While trowels are essentially outdoor tools, they can also be used indoors. Forks or spoons will serve the same purpose, but it is better not to compromise and invest in a trowel. There are specific trowels made for container gardens that will be useful. Using a trowel will allow you to get certain tasks done quickly and without stress.

Plant Stands

The matter of presentation is of concern when you have a container garden, especially if you are placing these containers around your home. It is better not to cram too many pots in the same spot. Instead, figure out an arrangement for the containers. Organize the pots around your house strategically. Getting a plant stand will help you arrange the plants on the shelves in an organized manner. It will usually have liners to hold any water that streams out from the container.

Plant Trays

A plant tray is an important accessory for container plants. These trays are also called drainage saucers or humidity trays. As you place your containers around your space, remember to put a plant tray below each container. This is a useful tool that you should not overlook when arranging your container garden.

Plant Stakes

Many plants cannot stand on their own. For these plants, you must provide stakes to support their growth. For instance, a climbing plant needs a stake to crawl upon. Stakes can be made of plastic, bamboo, or wood. You can also use wire tires. All of these will help your plant climb safely in the direction you set. A simple hack to use for small plants is to use bamboo skewers from your kitchen as stakes.

You now have the majority of the information you require to care for your container garden properly. Most people believe that simply planting a seed and watering it will grow a plant; however, there is much more to it, and remembering these points is the only way to grow healthy plants in your container garden. Container gardening differs from regular outdoor gardening in a few ways, which should be kept in mind. Following the recommendations in this section will make caring for your containers and container garden a breeze. It is a lot easier than you think, but it's not as simple as you think.

Chapter 6: Growing Pains

While gardening is a pleasure, it also comes with a few pains. However, a few growing pains are worth the extra trouble when you can reap the fruit of your efforts in the form of healthy plants all around your garden and home.

Gardeners must deal with the issue of pest control, regardless of the kind of garden they are growing. Container gardens can be a little easier to handle since they are more accessible, and problems can be identified and contained before they get out of hand. Taking a few steps to prevent pests and diseases will go a long way. But taking quick action when you notice an issue will help you take care of the problem before it spreads and kills your entire garden.

Tips to Ward off Pests from Your Container Garden

Potting Mix Should Not Be Reused

When you change the plant in your container, change the potting mix as well. This is especially important if the pot had previously housed a plant affected by bacteria or fungi. The soil may look reusable from a distance, but that disease may still be present, and this will be transferred to the next plant you use it for. Larvae or insect eggs are usually not clearly visible, so throw the soil out and use fresh potting mix.

Clean the Containers

Clean your containers well before you plant in them. This will prevent many issues in your container garden. Before each planting season, scrub out your containers with water and liquid detergent. If the container housed an infected plant, soak the pot in a mild bleach solution as an added precaution and thoroughly rinse it out before planting anything in it. Keep the cleaned pots out under the sun to air dry before storing them or using them again.

Buy Healthy Seeds, Seedlings, or Plants

When you buy seeds or plants, check that they are not already affected by some pest or disease. If you bring home an infected plant, you will only be causing more issues in your garden if the disease spreads.

Take Care of Your Plants

Keep the plants in your container garden well cared for and healthy by giving them adequate water, sunlight, and fertilizer. Healthier plants are better at warding off pests and disease. They are also better at recovering when affected by these issues. A sick plant is more prone to disease and may not survive long enough for you to treat it.

Not All Bugs Are Bad

Not every bug is a problem in your container garden. Some helpful bugs will help get rid of the harmful bugs. Some bugs may help promote the growth of healthy plants in other ways. For instance, ground beetles and ladybugs will eat a few of the bugs that may otherwise eat your plants. Many insects will pass through your garden looking for prey in the form of other insects. Identify these and get rid of the ones that may harm your garden.

Regular Inspection

You need to monitor your container garden regularly to get a head start on any pest or disease issues. The sooner you spot it, the quicker you can solve the problem. Do not forget to check the soil for any pests that may have burrowed underground.

Clean Area

The area around the garden should be kept clean. It becomes a breeding ground for pests and diseases if it is dirty, and this will soon affect your container garden.

How to Get Rid of Garden Pests without Using Chemicals

Gardening can be a challenging endeavor at times, especially when you have to deal with all kinds of pests trying to invade your garden. Keeping the pH levels of the soil balanced and keeping the soil healthy is one of the best ways to prevent most pest infestations. However, a healthy garden will still attract many garden pests such as beetles, raccoons, and other pests.

Some common pests in container gardens include aphids, caterpillars, red spider mites, mealy bugs, snails, vine weevils, and whiteflies.

Here are some great chemical-free ways to get rid of all those pesky creatures:

Garden Lime

Garden lime can be dusted over green beans to get rid of any Japanese beetles. If you spread a wide strip of it around the perimeter of your garden, it will also keep skunks, snakes, and raccoons away. Garden lime will give any of these critters a burning sensation in their mouth the moment they lick it. This will usually prompt them to leave your garden alone.

Feathered Friends

Birds eat insects, and you can enlist the help of these feathered friends to get rid of the insects in your garden. Build or install a birdbath in your garden and always keep it filled with fresh water. This will invite birds to your garden regularly. It will also prevent them from picking on your tomato plants. Erecting a bird feeder alongside the birdbath will also be helpful. Fill it with seeds from late autumn till early spring. The garden will be a bird-friendly zone, and they can feed on these seeds instead of attacking any of your plants. All the while, they will pluck any unwanted bugs off your plants, which will benefit your garden. Guinea fowl is a good option if your garden is prone to Japanese beetles, ticks, or hornworms. Chickens are not always a good option as they may eat your vegetables or scratch some plants.

Diatomaceous Earth

If you want a natural barrier to stink bugs and similar crawling insects, use food-grade diatomaceous earth. Sprinkle it below the vegetables or fruit growing on the ground. You can also sprinkle it over the leaves of the plants.

Pepper and Onion Mixture

Grasshoppers and aphids can completely ruin flowerbeds and vegetable gardens. Make a blend of two hot peppers, one small onion, and one mild green pepper. Mix this with a quart jar of clean water. Use a spray bottle to apply this on plants that attract these pests.

Cayenne Pepper

Your garden will be prone to cabbage loopers if you grow cabbage, kale, or Brussels sprouts. Mix two spoons of cayenne pepper into a quart of water and spray it onto the stems and leaves of the plants. Spray it on the ground directly surrounding your plant as well. The spicy solution will deter these creatures.

Fish Fertilizer

Corn plants always attract squirrels to your garden. Mix two spoons of liquid fish fertilizer in a gallon of water. Pour this into a spray bottle and start spraying it on your rows of corn to deter the squirrels from digging them up.

DIY Bug Spray

If you want to make your own chemical-free bug spray, mix some warm water with liquid dish soap. Shake well and spray around your garden.

Chopsticks

Erect a lot of chopsticks around your plants, like a barrier. This will keep your pets or any big pests from disturbing your plant bed when you first sow the seeds.

Blood Meal

Blood meal can be used to keep away deer. Scatter dried blood meal around the garden bed between the rows of vegetables. Do this weekly or every ten days. It also keeps groundhogs and rabbits away. The one drawback is that it will attract dogs. Sprinkle a little garden lime over the blood meal if you have a dog or there are dogs in your area, as this will keep them away.

Onions and Garlic

Garlic and onions are natural insect deterrents. Plant them between or around other plants, and they will keep insects away. Planting these around your fruit tree will also protect the base of the trees from borers who may otherwise drill in there.

Orange Tape

If moose are common in your area, get some bright orange tape and wrap it around the stakes that surround your garden. This usually keeps them away.

Chrysanthemums

Fleas, roaches, lice, ants, and bedbugs are other issues in gardens. You can often repel most of these pests by planting chrysanthemums in the garden or around your home.

Bush Beans

If you want to grow potatoes in your garden, you may have to deal with the Colorado potato beetle. One of the easiest ways to keep this pest away is to alternate rows of bush beans with your potato rows. The potatoes, in turn, will repel the Mexican bean beetle from affecting your bush beans.

Radish

For a garden with cucumbers, melons, peas, beans, and squash, radish plants are a great way to keep the beetles away.

Basil

For healthy tomato plants, plant some basil next to them. It will enhance the growth of the tomato plant, protect it from harmful insects, and give you an added ingredient for your salads.

Catnip

Cucumber and zucchini plants tend to attract cucumber beetles. You can plant some tansy and catnip with these plants, and it will greatly control the population of these creatures.

Rosemary

This aromatic herb is a great way to keep carrot flies, cabbage moths, and beetles away from your garden. Tansy will also discourage any aphids or ants from affecting your garden.

Petunia

Colorado potato beetles tend to stay away from potato and bean plants when you grow petunias near them.

Common Plant Diseases that Occur in Container Gardens

Plant disease names are frequently derived from the symptoms of the disease. Some diseases affect only a specific type of plant, while others only affect a specific portion of a plant. Some diseases, for example, may only damage the leaves of the plant, while others may affect the stem.

The following are some abiotic and fungal diseases that can affect your container garden:

Fungal Diseases

Many plant diseases are caused by fungi. These tips will help you identify, prevent, and treat some fungi-caused diseases.

Black Spot

https://pixabay.com/photos/tar-spot-disease-maple-tree-1728438/

Black spots will appear on the stem and leaves of a plant infested by black spot fungi. While it usually infects rose plants, it can also attack some other fruiting plants. If your area experiences frequent summer rain showers or warm and humid weather, keep a lookout for this disease in your container garden. The best way to prevent this disease is to plant a resistant variety in your garden. Another tip is to clean the pots regularly if you plant roses in them. When you prune your plants, get rid of the debris and throw out any fallen leaves. If some leaves turn yellow or show spots, cut them out. Overhead watering is to be avoided, and watering early in the morning is better as it will give the leaves a chance to dry off faster.

Botrytis Blight

This fungal disease is also called gray mold, and it is common on petunias, strawberries, and other flowering plants. If you see gray fuzz on old fruit or flowers, it may be the blight. Blight can also cause spots and discoloration. It tends to affect older parts of your plants and is more likely to occur in places where the weather is humid and cold. Keep your plants adequately spaced to prevent them from spreading the disease from one to another. Another way to prevent blight is by avoiding overhead watering. Any infected plant parts should be removed and destroyed.

Powdery Mildew

https://www.freepik.com/free-photo/nephthytis-plant-leaf-white-background_16238783.htm#page=7&query=powdery%20mildew%20plant%20disease&position=1&from_view=search&track=ais

If your plants are affected by this fungus, it will leave a white powder coating on the flowers and leaves. This issue is common where the days are warmer with cooler nights; it is a weather-dependent disease. Your plants might recover and grow normally if you can get them to grow through one cycle of the disease. It is difficult to control the spread of this disease. You can try spraying them with some neem oil, which acts as a natural repellant.

Damping Off

Damping off will cause the base of stems in seedlings to rot. This causes weakness, which leads to wilting, and it will then make the stem fall over. The simplest step to prevent this disease is to avoid overwatering and use sterile potting soil during planting. Alternatively, chamomile tea might be used. In four cups of boiling water, brew a chamomile tea bag overnight. Seeds can be soaked in the mixture for two hours before planting; seed trays and seedlings can be sprayed with it. Give a brief spritz with the tea if you notice white mold on the base of your seedlings or in the soil.

Rust

The symptom of this disease is the formation of rust-colored pustules on the lower side of the plant leaf. The upper sides will soon turn yellow, and, in a while, the entire plant will begin to rot away. Allow for good air circulation for your container plants by spacing them well. Keep your plants and garden clean, avoid overhead watering, and try mulching at the base of your plants. Any infected plant should be destroyed so it does not affect the other plants.

Abiotic Diseases

Plant diseases or problems not caused by organisms, such as bacteria or fungus, are called abiotic diseases. These diseases are usually caused by temperature, light, or other atmospheric conditions.

Sunburn

If the leaves on your plant appear bleached, it may be sunburn. Plants usually recover well from sunburn. You can avoid this by hardening your plants before exposing them to harsh elements.

Salt Burn

When there is an excessive buildup of fertilizer salts in the soil, it can cause salt burn. The edges of the leaves become yellowish and then brown due to the burn. At some point, the entire leaf will get dry and fall off. The tip of the branch may die as well. If you notice symptoms of salt burn in your plant, flood the soil with a lot of water. This is also a good way to wash out excessive salts when you add fertilizer. Let the water drain and repeat the process five-six times. You need to ensure that your containers have adequate drainage before you start flooding them with water.

Wind and Hail

Wind and hail tend to cause more damage to plants that have large, tender leaves. When the leaves are hit by wind and hail, they create open wounds on the plant leaves, creating an opening for fungal infections. This kind of damage cannot be reversed if severe. If it only affects a few leaves, you can pluck those off and dispose of them. However, if the entire plant is affected, you can only hope that it will recover independently. If it does not, remove the plant and clean out the container before replanting a replacement.

Frost Damage

If plants are affected by frost or very chilly weather, it experiences blackened foliage. This blackening tends to occur in the parts of the plant that are more exposed. If you are expecting a cold spell in your area, move your containers to a sheltered spot. If you cannot move them, use an old sheet to cover them until the chill passes. If the frost only affects the top leaves of your plants, pick off those leaves, and the plant will usually recover on its own.

Chapter 7: Container Herbs

Herbs are one of the most popular options for container gardens for various reasons. Having a small herb container garden just outside your kitchen or growing a few herbs in containers on your windowsill makes cooking a pleasure. Almost every kind of herb can be grown in containers. You can grow each herb in a different container or grow a few together in the same one. When mixing herbs, you need to ensure that you plant herbs with the same growing requirements together. This will make maintenance easy and allow the herbs to grow together well. For instance, some herbs may need more watering than others. They should be planted in different pots to avoid under watering or overwatering of either plant. If you properly manage the growing conditions, you will have a thriving herb garden in your home.

Starting Your Herb Container Garden

Use the following tips to get started with your first herb container garden:

Planning

One container can grow several herbs if they have the same growing requirements like the amount of water, sunlight exposure, etc. For instance, parsley cannot be grown with rosemary in the same container.

The former thrives in dry, hot conditions, while the latter needs constant moisture. This combination will not grow well in the same container.

Herbs can be grown to supplement your grocery list, but they are also a great decorative element to your container garden. They will add scent and texture to your garden when mixed with some perennials or annuals. But no matter what kind of plant you mix them with, check that they need similar growing conditions. Some herbs may choke out the other plant you grow them with and affect healthy plant growth.

Choose Containers for Your Herb Garden

Almost any kind of container can be used for growing herbs. You must, however, ensure that the container allows for good drainage. Since most herbs have small root systems, you can use small containers successfully. For instance, a tin can that previously stored baked beans can be used for growing an herb. Just clean it out and puncture a few holes at the bottom before adding potting mix. Herbs that can be dried out between watering sessions are good for small containers, too. The disadvantage of using small containers is that you can only put a limited amount of soil in them, and thus there is limited nutrition, and your watering needs to be more precise. You must continually check to see when the herbs need watering and be careful not to overwater.

Self-watering containers are suitable for herbs that require a constant water source. Use self-watering containers for herbs such as parsley, mint, chives, and marjoram. Do not grow herbs such as basil, oregano, and thyme in self-watering pots, as they require a drying period between each watering.

Planting and Caring for Your Herb Garden

You can help all your herbs thrive in their containers by providing them with the right soil, fertilizer, and amount of sunlight. Using a high-quality potting mix is recommended; also, ensure that it allows for proper drainage. Potting mix with good drainage and containers with drainage holes will prevent your herbs from drowning when you water them.

Most herbs thrive in less than 6–7 hours of sunlight every day. On a hot day, your container might just be a baking tray for your herbs. If your region's temperatures tend to soar at certain times of the day, move them to the shade for a while. Overexposure to heat and sunlight will do more harm than good.

It is also important to fertilize your herbs with the right amount of fertilizer. Herbs do not usually need much fertilizer, and some will die if you over-fertilize them. In fact, certain herbs, such as oregano and thyme, do better when you fertilize and water them minimally, and these conditions help them taste better as well.

Herb Harvesting

It is usually recommended that you harvest your herb plants often as it encourages them to branch out and fill their containers more. This allows you to increase the amount of harvest you get from each container. The harvesting pattern should be tailored to the growth pattern of the herb. Do not cut more than a third of your plant during its growing season. For instance, if you grow basil, harvest the herb regularly and remove the flower buds.

To harvest your herbs, simply snip and pinch back the section being harvested.

With herbs such as dill and chives, you can eat the seeds and flowers. For plants such as basil or oregano, the leaves get bitter when the plant can flower. Once your herb has flowered and gone to seed, its growth cycle for that season is complete, and it will not be putting out new growth.

If your home gets a lot of indoor sunlight, bring your herb pots into the shade after the growing season ends. Some herbs survive through the winter better when brought in. You can try this for nearly every herb before the cold weather hits your garden.

If your herb garden grows well, you might find yourself with a larger harvest than you need. Some herbs, such as sage, oregano, and rosemary, can be dried and kept for use throughout the year. Remember to keep them out of direct sunlight and enclosed in tightly lidded containers. For other herbs that cannot be stored, take the opportunity to give some to your friends or family so they do not go to waste.

Herbs Best Suited for Container Gardening

You can choose the herbs you wish to cultivate now that you know how to get started with your herb container garden. You can grow almost any herb in a container, so you have many options. Growing your own herbs has several advantages: you can pluck and use fresh herbs when cooking; you will not run out of herbs in the middle of a meal; you'll save money on groceries, and you'll be assured of high-quality products without the use of harmful chemicals because you'll be growing them yourself.

Here are the best herbs to grow in a container garden:

Greek Oregano

https://pixabay.com/photos/oregano-leaves-herbs-foliage-fresh-2662890/

Oregano tends to grow quite enthusiastically in any garden. Growing this herb in a container is a better option than directly growing it in the ground since the container gives you better control over its growth. The small leaves of the oregano plant are very flavorful and the perfect topping for bruschetta or pizza. You can also add some to your marinades and vinaigrettes.

Basil

https://pixabay.com/photos/basil-herbs-food-dew-932079/

Basil is one of the best herbs to grow in the summer, and there are many varieties to choose from, including Nufar, Genovese, or Dolce Fresca. This annual herb grows well in warm weather and will thrive when planted in containers like a window box. Some gardeners struggle to grow this plant well, but it is usually relatively easy if you give it a lot of sunshine and well-drained soil. Harvest it frequently and watch as it continues to push out new growth each time. If you notice any flower buds appearing, pinch them off. The flavor of the basil leaves will decline if the plant flowers.

Rosemary

https://pixabay.com/photos/branch-rosemary-blossom-bloom-1525050/

Rosemary can be grown as an annual herb, and the aromatic herb is a favorite worldwide. The woody shrub has needle-like foliage and is easy to grow. When the weather cools down and the days get shorter, you can simply move it near a sunny window instead of leaving it outside to wither. This increases its growing season. Most rosemary variants grow upright, but you can choose the ones that grow downward in the edges of your planters. If you live in a colder region, Arp is more tolerant to cold weather. For larger leaves, opt for Gorizia. Be careful of the amount of water you pour into this plant since it dries quickly from overwatering. While it needs consistent moisture, it does not do well when drenched.

Mint

Mint grows aggressively and is best suited for container gardens. If you plant some mint in the ground, you will find it growing all over, and it is very difficult to get rid of. Growing mint in a container gives you much more control over its growth and allows you to restrain it to that pot. There are many different mint varieties to choose from; spearmint, mojito mint, strawberry mint, etc. You can grow a few different varieties in the same pot, and they will thrive well. Mix one part of the compost mixture with two parts of potting soil before you plant the mint. Ensure that the soil is rich and that there is always ample moisture for your plant. This herb is a great summer ingredient for everything from salads to drinks.

Thyme

https://pixabay.com/photos/thyme-herbs-culinary-herbs-cook-1781005/

If you want to grow a very low-maintenance herb, choose thyme. It is drought tolerant and will survive even if you briefly neglect it. If you grow thyme with other herbs, plant it in the front half, so the tiny leaves can attractively grow over the edge. Avoid overwatering since it grows better when the soil is a bit dry and is drought resistant. Ensure that it gets a lot of sunlight. English thyme is one of the best kinds for culinary use since it has a bold lemon flavor and scent.

Lemon Balm

Lemon balm is a hardy perennial that grows aggressively like mint. This herb can quickly take over the space it is planted in; it is better suited for a contained space. Planting lemon balm in a separate container is the best way to control its growth. Mix one part compost with two parts of potting soil before you plant the herb. It requires regular watering as lemon balm needs moist soil. The herb is very flavorful and will add the smell and taste of lemons to any dish.

Parsley

Parsley is another must-have in a culinary herb container garden. The flat-leaved and curly varieties are a favorite of most gardeners. You can add the curly parsley variety to a planter with other ornamentals, such as geraniums or petunias. This herb is relatively easy to grow, but you must water it regularly and provide enough fertilizer. The best way to ensure it gets proper nutrition is by using a slow-release organic fertilizer when you plant the herb. While this herb loves full sunlight, it can also do well under a bit of shade.

Chives

Chives will grow well in a container garden and are a hardy perennial in zones 3–10. You can grow this plant outdoors all throughout the year. This grassy herb has hollow leaves and can reach a height of about twenty inches in a pot. Although this herb is essential, like tiny onions, the bulbs are not used, and instead, the blooms and leaves are harvested. You can also consume the pinkish-purple flowers. The soil in the container must be rich in organic matter and a well-draining kind. This herb thrives under the full sun but will tolerate light shade, too.

Cilantro

https://pixabay.com/photos/parsely-green-healthy-meal-plant-1688651/

Cilantro is also called coriander and is an annual herb. The herb is grown for its seeds and tangy leaves. It thrives under full sunlight but can tolerate a little shade. You must use a container with more depth since it has a long taproot. Certain cilantro varieties will grow nearly two feet tall in their pots.

Lavender

Lavender is a perennial that grows best under full sunlight. This bushy shrub needs well-drained potting soil. Avoid overwatering as it does better in drier soil. Avoid fertilizing this herb, too. The hardiness of the plant will depend on what variety you grow. Certain types of lavender will grow up to a height of two feet in their containers.

Tarragon

The bold flavor of this herb is why it gets its name, which means little dragon in French. Use well-drained soil and place the pot under full sunlight. The plant can grow nearly three feet tall if you care for it well. It is a low-maintenance herb and drought resistant. Avoid overwatering this plant. It can be grown as a hardy perennial in zones 5–9.

Lemon Verbena

https://pixabay.com/photos/lemon-verbena-herbs-plant-74350/

This annual herb grows well in containers and should be placed under full sun. It is a tropical shrub and needs well-drained soil. Do not use fertilizer while planting lemon verbena since it grows better with minimal nutrients.

Sage

Sage comes in a few different varieties that grow well under full sun. It needs a well-drained potting mix, but you must keep the soil moist. Sage is a great seasoning for poultry dishes. This herb can grow up to a couple of feet and is usually hardy in zones 4-10.

Marjoram

Marjoram is a relative of oregano but with a milder, sweeter aroma and flavor. It should be planted in a well-drained potting mix and kept under full sun. The perennial grows well in zones 8-10. The herb can grow to nearly two feet tall if nurtured. Bring it indoors before the winter frost hits, and it will give you harvest even through the winter.

Chapter 8: Fruit in Pots

Container Gardening for Fruit Trees

It is surprisingly easy to grow fruit trees in a container garden. In fact, growing a fruit tree in a container instead of a conventional garden has certain advantages. If you grow a small fruit tree, it can easily be moved around your yard, patio, or deck according to the light and shade available. If your garden soil is not suitable for some fruit trees, you can grow them in a container with the appropriate medium. Container gardening is also quite suitable for growing fruit trees that may be borderline hardy in your area. You must keep in mind that a potted tree will usually give smaller quantities of fruit than a garden tree. The advantage is that the potted tree can give you fruit ready for harvesting earlier than the ground-grown alternative. Growing a fruit tree in a container garden is not as difficult as some people expect. There is a bit of a learning curve, but you will reap the fruit of your labor if you use the following tips:

- **Plant the Dwarf or Semi-Dwarf Variety**

Full-sized fruit trees are usually challenging to grow in a container. Most of these trees are available in a dwarf or semi-dwarf variety. You can move these trees to bigger pots as they grow. Replanting in bigger pots along the course of the life of your tree is important, or the fruit production will reduce.

The following are the best fruit tree options in dwarf varieties for a container garden:

Cherries

This tree is grown for its summer fruit and spring blossoms. If you want your cherry harvest to be sweet, these plant varieties will need a lot of sunlight. Sour cherry trees will grow under shade, though. Since these trees have shallow roots, they must be watered thoroughly for a year after planting. You must ensure proper water supply during a dry spell.

Apples

You can get an apple tree that is grafted on a dwarf rootstock. Choose the self-fertile kind where different varieties are grafted together if you are only growing one tree.

Peaches and Nectarines

Container gardens work well for dwarf varieties of this fruit. They are cold-sensitive, so you can protect them by moving them indoors or under a shelter before winter hits. Bonanza and Pixy are good varieties for you to try growing.

Plums

Plum trees need well-drained soil, so add some perlite or sand to your potting mix while planting. Pixy is a good dwarf variety of this plant. Growing it in containers allows you to protect the early blossoms by moving the plant to a sheltered spot.

Raspberries

This cane fruit blooms in autumn and summer bearing varieties. When grown in pots, the plant forms some long canes, but it is not a tree plant. The variety that bears fruit in the summer will not be as bushy as the autumn-bearing kind. Therefore, the former is more suitable for small container gardens. Glen Moy is a good variety of raspberry plants for new gardeners.

- **Use the Right Kind of Soil**

The type of soil you use for growing your fruit trees in containers is an important factor affecting their growth. The potting soil used in the pot will often determine how much watering is required as well. Most high-quality potting mixes will be suitable for a container-grown tree. If you do not buy a readymade mix, you can create your own. Just mix equal parts peat moss, sand, and vermiculture. Perlite can also be used instead of vermiculture. If the soil is right, a fruit tree requires the same care as any other plant in a container garden.

- **Choose Quality Pots**

If you want your pots to last and want a thriving garden, invest in quality pots. For fruit trees, get pots with at least ten–fifteen inches of depth so that their roots have space for growth. Cheap plastic pots will soon get faded, and unless you are often repotting, the tree will be growing in that pot for a long time. Good-quality polyurethane pots or glazed ceramic pots are a good option.

- **Overwinter**

Fruit trees can be overwintered in cooler regions around the country. Fruit trees are not always zone-hardy, and as a result, container growth is a good option. This way, you can move the tree to places where the temperature is suitable, even in winter. For instance, unheated garages tend to stay warm for more extended periods. The potted trees must be watered thoroughly before they are moved to a sheltered location. While most fruit trees can be overwintered, you should not overwinter citrus trees. They usually need to go into dormancy for a period during winter and should be left outside.

- **Proper Watering and Feeding**

Growing media in pots usually needs extra fertilizer after a while because the fruit tree will consume nutrients as it grows. To feed the plant properly, use a good slow-release fertilizer to ensure the fruit tree remains healthy. But over-fertilization can also be a problem, so follow the instructions on the fertilizer label accordingly. Fertilizers for fruit trees should have a high nitrogen content and many trace minerals. When summer starts, it is also vital to water frequently. Since watering can wash nutrients out of the potting mix, you should water the fruit trees frequently and fertilize them more frequently. Most potted plants left in the sun will require frequent watering in hot weather since the soil dries up faster. Containers made of clay and porous material can also dry out the soil faster than other containers. The simplest way to check if the soil is moist is by sticking a finger into the second knuckle. If the soil feels dry, the plant must be watered; however, the potting medium should be kept moist and not soggy. The pots should always allow for the drainage of excess water.

- **Buy Fruit Trees from Reputable Sellers**

While your own efforts matter, the quality of the plant you use will also play a role in determining whether you succeed. Find reputable sellers from whom you can source your fruit trees, or any other plant, for that matter. Buying plants grown from bad seeds, diseased plants, or those grown in low-quality soil will affect the way your fruit tree grows.

Fruit to Grow in Container Gardens

Here is a list of some other fruit to start growing in your container garden:

Strawberries

One of the best fruits to grow in your container garden is strawberry. These perennial plants only need to be planted once, and if you take care of them, they will bear fruit for years to come. Choose the everbearing variety for your containers as it will give you the chance to harvest twice a year. Everbearing strawberry plants will bear fruit in June and late summer. This will also prevent your garden from getting overrun at once. For every ten–twelve strawberry plants, you will need a pot about twenty inches wide. This fruit needs at least eight hours of full sun for good growth. Ensure that the pots have good drainage as well.

Blueberries

It is a little different when it comes to growing blueberries in containers. For a decent harvest, you will have to grow about two–three plants. These will bear fruit from June to August. Use pots that are about eighteen–twenty inches deep and have a diameter of about twenty-two inches. The soil should be acidic and peat-based. These two factors will help you grow a decent harvest of blueberries in your container garden.

Figs

https://pixabay.com/photos/figs-fruits-fresh-ripe-organic-2079166/

If you like figs, try growing some in your containers. You only need a pot that has a diameter of about sixteen inches. This plant is not very picky with the soil it grows in, but you must ensure that it has proper drainage. They are a drought-tolerant plant, but it needs full sun. In summer, regular watering is important since the soil dries out faster from exposed containers.

Cantaloupe

https://pixabay.com/photos/cantaloupe-mushmelon-melon-fruit-59168/

The taste of a fresh cantaloupe grown in your container garden will beat any store-bought fruit. You need to plant this fruit tree in a large container to accommodate the fruit. The growing process is the same as how you would grow it in a regular garden. Make sure that you use a stick or trellis to give the vines and fruit support.

Pineapple

The next time you buy a pineapple, cut off the crown and soak it in water for a couple of days. Plant this crown in a large container and place it under the sun. Regular watering and feeding will soon give you a pineapple grown in your very own container garden.

Bananas

You do not need to live in a tropical country to grow bananas. Banana plants come in a dwarf variety, too, and can be grown in containers. This perennial tree only needs to be planted once and will give you multiple harvests if you take care of it. Pruning the plant and bringing it indoors during winter will prevent it from being affected by frost. Use a large container with good drainage; this will prevent the plant from drying. You can move the container around easily, and growing your own bananas saves on your grocery bills.

Currants

https://pixabay.com/photos/currant-fruits-white-currants-550600/

It is easy to grow currants in a container, and they do not need too much effort. Get a large pot and mix a good amount of compost into the potting mix. Once you plant it, water it regularly, and watch as it grows. You will soon have many homegrown currants for your currant jam.

Watermelon

Did you know that watermelons can be grown in containers, too? Growing this plant in a container is not too difficult, and it helps you control the vine growth in your garden. It needs a lot of sunlight, but you can grow the plant indoors or outdoors. Direct sunlight is not compulsory, so you can place the pot under a window or even provide artificial sunlight.

Mulberries

Buy the dwarf variety and plant a few together in a large pot. They are easy to grow, but the drawback of this plant is that the ripe fruit leaves stains. Do not let it grow directly on your porch or patio, and keep a plate, or some other holder, below it to catch the fruit.

Gooseberries

Growing gooseberries is like growing currants. Get a large container and use the same kind of soil and fertilizer that you would for your currants.

Tips for Growing Fruit in Containers

- Add fertilizer to your plant every couple of weeks since potted plants do not have the same access to nutrients as ground plants do.

- Make sure that your containers have drainage holes, or the fruit tree might drown.

- Check the sunlight requirement of the fruit you grow and make sure your container is placed accordingly. While some fruit trees require long hours of sunlight, others grow well in the shade or under only a few hours of sunlight.

- Avoid overcrowding the plants in one pot. A single plant can give rise to a couple more in the same pot, so keep that in mind when planting.

- Find out how big the fruit tree is supposed to grow so you can monitor its growth. If it is not growing the way it is supposed to, you can adjust the nutrients, watering cycle, etc.

- Use the right size of pot according to the plant you are growing. Some fruit trees will require a deeper and wider pot, while others do well in shallow containers.

Chapter 9: Vegetables That Thrive in Containers

In this chapter, we talk about growing vegetables that grow exceptionally well when farmed in containers. Since vegetables are a more popular container garden choice, we have listed several common vegetables you may want to grow. We also tell you what each vegetable needs regarding watering, pruning, harvesting, and what it needs from its container (i.e., tomatoes may need a cage, and potatoes may need a special pot that allows for access without disturbing the plant). This section will highlight specific plant hybrid varieties that are good for containers, such as "patio tomatoes" versus just saying, "Tomatoes are great for container farming." You will learn what vegetables are easiest to grow and what ones can prove to be a little more difficult for new gardeners.

Container Sizes for Vegetables

If you want to grow vegetables on your balcony, rooftop, or patio, you must ensure that the containers are big enough to support the plant's size. The container should hold enough soil and moisture for nutrient delivery to allow for healthy plant growth. It should allow the plant to leaf, flower, and finally bear fruit, or, in this case, vegetables. The pot must also be large enough to accommodate the plant's root system. The pot should be large enough to prevent the container from tipping over due to the weight and height of the plant growing above ground. A little pot may not be able to support your plant if it becomes too big or heavy above the soil. While some plants are small enough to be cultivated in a single container, others require their own pot to allow their rapid growth. When planting these plants, use a separate container.

If the depth of the container is at least eight inches, it will usually be able to hold enough soil, moisture, and nutrients to promote the growth of most kinds of vegetables and herbs. These usually need to be watered about three times a week. If you use a smaller container, the watering schedule will have to be more frequent, and so will the frequency of fertilizing.

Here are the suggested container sizes for some common vegetables that you may want to grow in your container garden:

1. Mustard or Mizuna: use eight-inch containers for these Asian leaves.

2. Arugula: eight-inch containers are a good option for growing Arugula. You can plant this in your window box.

3. Broccoli: a single young plant should be grown in a five- or ten-gallon container.

4. Asparagus: a two-gallon pot will hold two of these plants. A ten-gallon container can accommodate five of these plants.

5. Beans: the pot needs to have about ten inches of soil depth for any bean. Bush beans should be planted about nine inches apart. Pole beans should be planted at least four inches apart. A ten-gallon pot will hold two plants.

6. Cabbage: a two-gallon pot can be used to grow one large head. A four–five-gallon container can be used to plant two heads, but the weaker one should be thinned out after a couple of weeks. Three large cabbage heads will need a ten-gallon pot.

7. Beets: a three-gallon container can grow seven beet plants, while a ten-gallon container can accommodate two dozen of these plants. Each plant should have a gap of two inches between it and any adjacent plant.

8. Bok choy: this plant needs an eight-inch container for one sapling.

9. Carrots: for a container garden, choose varieties according to the container. A two-gallon container will be suitable for carrots that mature when they grow to about four inches. Five-gallon containers are used for growing carrots maturing to six inches. Ten-gallon containers are used for growing carrot varieties growing to about ten inches. Thinning should be done, so allow for two-inch gaps between the carrots. The tip of the root should not touch the bottom of your container. This will prevent the carrot from growing to maturity.

10. Celery: a two-gallon container can grow one celery plant. A ten-gallon container will comfortably house five plants.

11. Cauliflower: a container of three–five gallons will grow one plant. If you have a ten-gallon container, grow up to three plants in it.

12. Chicory: to grow three chicory plants, use an eighteen-inch container.

13. Chard: a two-gallon pot can grow a single plant, while a ten-gallon pot will accommodate five plants.

14. Collards: a two-gallon container is suitable for two plants, and a five-gallon container will grow four plants.

15. Chives: when planting a seed, use a three-inch container. Once it grows, replant in an eight-inch pot.

16. Corn: this crop will need a container with at least eight inches of soil depth. A fifteen-gallon container can grow three plants, while six standard-size ones can be grown in a pot double that size. For growing bantam-type corn, use a fifteen-gallon pot to grow six plants. Each plant should have a gap of at least four inches between it and adjacent plants.

17. Eggplant: a single plant can be grown in a five-gallon pot. A ten-gallon pot will accommodate up to three of these plants.

18. Cucumber: a five-gallon container can be used to grow one compact cucumber plant. The standard variety can be grown by planting three in a ten-gallon container.

19. Endive: use an eighteen-inch container for these plants and thin them out to maintain an eight-inch gap between them.

20. Horseradish: the container should be five gallons or larger since this plant is deep-rooted.

21. Garlic: use a five-gallon pot and plant cloves with about three inches of space between each one.

22. Kale: a single plant will need a one-gallon container, but two plants will need a five-gallon pot. Plants will need thinning when grown together and should be at least sixteen inches apart.

23. Jicama: use a five-gallon container for one plant.

24. Kohlrabi: use an eight-inch container for a single plant.

25. Lettuce: the container for lettuce plants should be big enough to allow a ten-inch gap during thinning.

26. Leeks: a five-gallon container can be used to grow eighteen plants. The container should have a depth of fourteen inches or more.

27. Mustard greens: eight-inch pots should be used for this plant. Thinning should allow a four-inch distance between each plant.

28. Peas: use a ten-gallon container for the climbing or bush-type pea. A planter or window box is suitable. There should be a gap of two inches between each plant. Wire trellis will help to support plant growth.

29. Melon: use a five-gallon container for one plant and a ten-gallon container for two plants.

30. Okra: a ten-gallon container should be used for one plant.

31. Peppers: for growing a large plant, use a three-gallon pot. Smaller plants do not need as much space. There should be twelve inches of space between the plants.

32. Onions: avoid crowding while planting seeds or sets. Use a twenty-four-inch pot, and it should have at least ten inches of depth. In the case of green onions, the container can be shallower.

33. Roach: use a twelve-inch pot for one plant.

34. Pumpkins: use a five-gallon container or larger for one pumpkin.

35. Potatoes Potato plants need containers that are at least twelve inches in depth and width. Use a five-gallon container for planting five seeds. Ten seed potatoes can be grown in a ten-gallon container. Whisky barrels are a great option for this plant.

36. Rhubarb: one plant will need a container larger than ten gallons.

37. Radish: the pot must be at least eight inches deep, and the plants need to have a couple of inches between them.

38. Scallions: use an eighteen-inch pot, and thinning should allow for two inches between each plant.

39. Rutabaga: a twenty-gallon container will accommodate fifteen plants.

40. Sorrel: use a twelve-inch container for this plant.

41. Spinach: use a two-gallon container for three plants and a ten-gallon one for ten plants. Thinning should allow for five inches between the plants.

42. Sweet potatoes: a twenty-gallon container should be used for sweet potatoes.

43. Squash: the container should be five gallons or larger for one squash plant. For a couple of vining plants, a ten-gallon container should be used.

44. Tomatoes: the large majority of species can be grown in a ten-gallon container for one plant, but bigger is better. A five-gallon container will help you grow miniature tomatoes. You can start with seeds in a three-inch container and then replant in a five-inch container. This potting up should be continued until you can move the plant outside.

45. Swiss chard: use a twelve-inch, or larger, container for Swiss chard. Thin them out with an eight-inch gap between each plant.

46. Zucchini: use a fifteen-inch pot for one plant.

47. Turnips: use a twenty-gallon container for fifteen plants.

Drainage is an important factor for container gardens to flourish. If the container has a diameter of fewer than ten inches, the drainage hole should be at least half an inch in diameter. For larger containers, there should be three–four drainage holes.

While you can cultivate all of the plants indicated above in your container garden, some are more suited and easier to grow than others. The vegetables outlined below are the best for container gardening.

Best Vegetables to Grow in Containers

TomatoesTomatoes are an easy vegetable to grow, and it can be incredibly satisfying to see them sprout in your plant. While they are technically a fruit, we will list them under vegetables here. Most varieties of tomatoes prefer a large container and need a tomato cage or staking. This helps support the fruit that is heavy and avoids having the vines bend or break. If you plant seedlings, use the short, stocky ones without blossoms. The larger the variety of tomatoes you want to grow, the bigger the pot you should use. For small cherry tomatoes, you do not need as much soil or space in the container. Don't move this plant out too early as it does not do well in cold weather. Hardening or acclimating the seedlings gradually will help them to grow well once you move them out. While planting, seed leaves should be removed from the seedling, along with the first true leaf set. Plant half of the seedling below the soil since tomatoes are usually planted deeper than most other plants. The leaves are toxic for pets, so they should be kept inaccessible. Tomatoes need full sun and moist soil with good drainage. They can be grown in all zones as an annual plant.

Atlas Hybrid Tomato

This is the first beefsteak hybrid variety of tomato that was designed for container growth. It is great for growing on the porch or deck under the warm sunlight. It is a beautiful tomato variety that is compact and gives a large bounty of one-pound tomatoes.

Bush Early Girl Hybrid Tomato

This hybrid is a fast-growing bushy variant. After planting, you can harvest large, sweet tomatoes within 70 days. This variety will support itself and just needs some full sun.

Potato

Potatoes you buy at the grocery store are not half as good as freshly picked potatoes from your garden. The water content in fresh potatoes is higher, and they have an earthier, bitter flavor. You will need a lot of soil and water for growing potatoes in a container, but the result is well worth the effort. Potatoes need full sun and loamy soil that is well drained. You also need to provide extra protection from fungus or blight, which can easily affect this ground plant.

Beets

Beets are perfect for growing in small containers; however, they need more depth than width to grow well. The pot should allow for adequate root growth, but otherwise, most varieties grow well in a container garden.

Chioggia Beet

This beet has candy stripes where you see red and white rings alternate from the outside to the center of the beet. Cut it in half, and you can easily see this pattern. This variety takes 55 days before you can harvest mature beets. It is best suited for some partial shade, so keep the pots in a shaded balcony or patio. The taste is sweeter than other beet varieties.

Detroit Dark Red Beet

This variety gives you sweet beets that are deep red in color. You can harvest them when they mature, or even as young roots. The matured beets grow to about three inches and take about two months to mature. Provide it with full sun to support good growth.

Peas

Plan for peas in early spring or the fall when the weather gets cooler. You can choose from snow peas, sugar peas, and English peas for your containers. This plant is a great option for succession planting since they add nitrogen to the soil. This will make the soil more fertile for the next plant. Peas should be planted in early spring and pulled out once the weather gets warmer. Use the same soil for planting something else since the soil from the pea plant will naturally fertilize other plants and enrich them with nitrogen, which is vital for growth. While planting and caring for peas, get your children involved since it is an "easy" plant that grows quickly. It needs full sun and loamy or enriched soil. It grows well in zones 2–11; just ensure good drainage.

Squash

Another easy container garden vegetable is squash. The blossoms from this plant are also edible and look beautiful in any garden. They need ample room to grow, and you need to use a large container. Ideally, this plant should get a lot of light and rich soil. Feeding and watering need to be done consistently. Do not choose the giant variety of this plant since it can weigh a lot and can topple your container over. Instead of winter squash, opt for the Honey bear variety of acorn squash or tiny pumpkin varieties. This vegetable is suitable for zones 3–10.

Peppers

Hot and sweet peppers are beautiful additions to your garden. The purple and orange peppers look especially attractive. You need large containers to grow peppers, but they are especially suited for grow boxes. If they get a lot of sun, moist soil, and good drainage, they will flourish. While you need to water them consistently, the soil should never be too wet or left dry. Planting peppers in a container makes it easy to move the plant inside when there is too much rain. You can choose from all kinds of shapes, sizes, and colors when buying pepper varieties. The range of spices of hot peppers also varies, so you can grow the kind that suits your taste buds. This plant grows annually in all growing zones.

Confetti Hybrid Peppers

These peppers are petite but are a treat for your taste buds. The green striped peppers ripen to red and look beautiful. Their small size makes them ideal for containers, and they can be harvested within 60 days. This variety does not need extra support and grows best under full sun.

Jungle Parrot Pepper

The tiny size but high yields from this hybrid pepper variety makes it perfect for patio containers. The peppers are sweet and colorful and are around two inches in size. They grow best under full sun and can be picked within 80 days.

Salad Greens

Salad greens like lettuce can be quickly grown in containers. Growing these in containers will give you much more control over weeds and pests than growing them in the ground. These are spring plants by nature, but newer varieties have been developed to withstand the summer heat. Another way of extending the harvest season for salad greens is by moving the containers to a cooler spot with shade once the temperature rises. Unlike most other vegetables, lettuce requires partial sunlight. Provide it with fertile, moist soil, and you can grow it easily in zones 4-9.

Bloomsdale Long Standing Spinach

This spinach variety will give you an abundant harvest of deep green, delicious leaves. They adapt well to all sun and shade and can be harvested upon maturing at around 50 days.

Okinawa

Okinawa is a leafy perennial that is better known as a spinach variety since it is similar. It acts as an ornamental plant as the undersides of its leaves are a beautiful purple. It takes very little time to care for this plant, and it is a healthy addition to your diet; it helps lower bad cholesterol levels. This variety is native to Indonesia, but you can grow it, too, if you keep the pot in a sunny spot.

Cucumbers

Cucumbers grow quickly in containers. This plant loves water, so you need to use pots made of plastic or ceramic, which will retain moisture in the soil. They also love heat, so they are an ideal plant for container growth. The temperature of the soil in a container rises faster than that of soil in the ground. Choose between bush and vining cucumbers and then decide on a variety depending on the end use of the plant. Certain varieties are better for pickling, while others are better for salads. Bush cucumbers usually give a smaller yield, and you need to provide a tomato cage or trellis for vining cucumbers. Ensure that the plant gets enough light and keep the soil moist and enriched with fertilizer. Cucumbers grow well in zones 4-12.

Arugula

Arugula leaves and flowers are both tasty edibles. This plant does not need a very big container, but it needs around six hours of full sun with a little shade. Growing it in containers makes it easy to move the plant, which is great as it does not like scorching afternoon heat. Let it soak under the morning sunlight and move it to partial shade in the afternoon. The soil should be moist, and the container should allow for good drainage. Arugula is best suited for growing zones 3-11.

Slow Bolt Arugula

The peppery taste of this variety is quite distinctive, and it is a great ingredient in salads or sandwiches. The narrow, elongated leaves look like dandelion leaves. It is an edible annual best suited for cooler weather. Grow it under some shade, or use row covers for your containers if you keep them outside. This variety does better in summer than others since it is relatively resilient. It will also give you produce for a longer time.

Radish

Another quick-growing vegetable in container gardens is radish. A seed can be planted and harvested within a month. This plant does not need much space; use containers with about four–six inches depth. They are not suited for hot weather, and growing them in containers makes it easy to move them to cool spots as required. Adding a little water when temperatures rise will also help the plant cool down. Radishes come in many varieties; choose your seeds depending on what flavor and appearance you prefer. Radish greens and pods are also edible, making them a great addition to any kitchen container garden. Radish grows well in zones 2-10.

Solaris Hybrid Radish

This hybrid will give you small, round radishes that are a bright red color. If this plant is grown in the right conditions, it can be harvested throughout the year. It grows fast and can be picked in three weeks.

Cherry Belle Radish

This is a popular variety since it grows fast and is easy to care for. You can place the container indoors or outdoors, and it will grow well regardless of shade or sun. The radish is delicious and mild and matures within three weeks.

Eggplant

Eggplant is a great edible and ornamental plant to grow. Some varieties are heavy and dense so avoid growing those in containers. Hansel and Fairytale eggplants are compact cultivars that are better suited for pots. They taste great and look beautiful as well. You must use large containers that will support the bush-like growth and roots of the plant. Use pots that will retain moisture for longer but also have good drainage. Eggplants need full sun, and they are suited for growing in zones 5-12.

Onions

Onions grow well in containers, and this is especially true for green onions. Since these are a staple in most meals, this is a must-have for your container garden.

Tokyo Long White Onion

This variety gives you thin, long onions, which are ideal for pots. They mature anywhere between 60–100 days. These scallions are resistant to smut, pink root, and thrips.

White Lisbon Onion

It is a mild variety that does not have a bulb. It grows fast and does not take up too much room in a container. You can plant this variety more densely in a container than most other plants. In two months, you can harvest the young plants, but they take four months to mature. These onions thrive under full sun.

Chapter 10: Happily, Contained Flowers

In this chapter, we have listed different types of flowers that are best for container gardening. It also discusses the pairing of early spring, mid-summer, and late summer blooms. It will teach you how to water, prune, and clip your flowers, and explain the blooming season for each flower—this last part is most important as it helps gardeners learn what flowers to pair in pots if they want blooms for the whole season. You will also receive some tips on budget-friendly container flower gardening.

Flowers that Bloom Well in Container Gardens

You will be spoilt for choice when it comes to choosing flowers for your pots. Many different flowers grow well in pots, and their beautiful colors add beauty to any container garden or home. The following flowers are suitable for containers and are easy to grow for beginners.

Azaleas

https://pixabay.com/photos/azalea-spring-flower-nature-plant-5012549/

Azaleas are impressive flowering bushes that bloom in the summer. The flowers are large and colorful, and they last for weeks. This makes them a great option for vase displays. Azaleas are commonly grown in most southern-style gardens and usually appear as a large bush. If you want to grow them in your window boxes, you must prune them back a bit to prevent overgrowth. In fact, pruning can make them look like a flowering tree. Azaleas come in many hybrids, varieties, and species. Depending on the flower shape or color you want, you have many choose from.

Celosia

https://pixabay.com/photos/celosia-flower-bloom-blossom-6402590/

Celosia flowers are also known as cockscombs or wool flowers. The unusual flowers can bloom for nearly ten weeks and come in pink, red, gold, or purple. You can also find bicolored varieties of Celosia. The name means "burning" in Greek, and the plant got this name because the flowers look like fire when they bloom next to each other. The flower also looks like a rooster's comb, hence the name cockscomb. There are many other varieties. The flower keeps producing tiny seeds, which will give you new flowers in your container without much work.

Calla Lilies

Calla lily is also called Lily of the Nile. The flowers are usually a waxy white, and they curl and twist gracefully as they end in one delicate point. The flowers may also be red, pink, or orange. The heart-shaped foliage also has a variety of white spots. This plant is native to South African marshlands but is popularly grown as a container or pond plant in the United States. It can easily be grown in a container and usually reaches a height of two feet.

Chamomile

https://pixabay.com/photos/chamomile-flowers-plant-3489847/

Chamomile is a small white-petalled bloom that you can grow and dry to use as an herbal tea. It is said to have a calming effect, but for that, grow the German variety. The plant is around nine inches tall but can grow to about two feet. These beautiful flowers are simple yet great for any container garden.

Daffodils

https://pixabay.com/de/photos/narzissen-blumen-garten-pflanzen-3349706/

Daffodils, also known as Narcissus, are flowering plants that bloom in spring; however, certain species also bloom in autumn. Commonly, the flowers are either white or yellow. The flowers have six floral leaves surrounding a trumpet. They may also have a trumpet in yellow and white outer petals.

Chrysanthemum

Also known as mums, chrysanthemums come in many colors and varieties that grow well in container gardens. The two main types to consider are florist and hardy chrysanthemums. The hardy kind does better in cool weather, and you can overwinter it outside. The florist kind is more delicate and needs more attention. The latter will give you beautiful blooms that make it worth your time. These flowers are often the last to bloom in a garden before winter.

Dahlias

Dahlias come in dwarf and low-growing varieties that are suited for containers. The pot should be at least a foot in width and height. There are many different kinds of dahlias, so you can find them to match your taste. Other than blue, you can usually find dahlias in all colors.

Dianthus

Dianthus flowers add a dash of color to any garden and are perfect for containers. They come in many colors, such as red, white, pink, yellow, or purple, and some flowers are bicolored or marked on the petals. The plant can grow up to three feet, but there are smaller kinds, too. Any gardener can find a variety suited for their garden.

Daisies

Daisies are a beautiful addition to any home. The yellow-centered flower with white petals is easy to grow and has its own charm. Other varieties come in pink or purplish-red. They bloom from around early spring until the end of autumn. The common daisy is the typical daisy flower, but other flowers are known as daisies as well.

Foxgloves

The common foxglove is a beautiful plant that has cascading, trumpet-like blooms. They come in many colors ranging from white to pink to gray. The colors will depend on the variety of foxglove, and some even have spots inside the flowers.

Lavender

If you want a naturally aromatic flower in your home, grow some lavender. This plant has beautiful flowers in a unique purplish-blue shade. They add height to your container garden and are a great ornamental flower that grows well with vegetables or herbs. Lavender also attracts insects that are beneficial to the garden. Like chamomile, lavender buds can be dried to last longer, which can be used for potpourri.

Geraniums

Common geraniums will bloom between mid-spring and the beginning of fall. The flowers are about five inches wide and grow in clusters. They come in red, pink, purple, or white. It is a common container garden flower and is easy to grow.

Marigolds

Marigolds are commonly seen in butterfly gardens as they attract butterflies. They come in beautiful shades of white, orange, or yellow, and their odor helps keep away undeniable insects from your container garden. If you are growing eggplants, tomatoes, or potatoes, place the marigold pot next to their container. These flowers can help deter certain pests that may otherwise harm these vegetables.

Orchids

Moth orchids are the most grown orchid flowers in homes. You can choose from thousands of orchid varieties, but most of them are very difficult to care for. Your best bet for a container garden is a moth orchid plant. They are easy to grow and keep alive; however, you must understand that caring for orchids is different from how you care for your other container plants. Do your research on the orchid variety you choose to grow and follow up with consistent care.

Peonies

These large, colorful flowers are easy to grow and have a wonderful scent. The plant has a deep root system, so you need to grow them in containers with extra depth. Once the peonies are established, they do not need much maintenance; however, you need to ensure there is enough room for the root system not to affect the growth. You can choose from many varieties of peonies that come in red, white, pink, orange, or purple. They bloom around late spring or in early summer.

Pansies

Pansies are a hybrid flower plant that was developed in the early 1800s in England. They are hardy and bloom quickly since humans breed them selectively. You can choose from gold, orange, purple, white, or red pansies. They are easy to take care of and will do well in your container garden.

Petunias

Petunias are a classic flower that comes in colors like white, blue, and pink. The different varieties of this plant will give you different sizes of flowers as well. Grandiflora are large petunias, while hedgiflora are ground cover types. Milliflora will give you small flowers that survive harsh weather, and multiflora gives smaller blooms.

Roses

One of the most beloved and grown flowers in the world is the rose. They come in all kinds of shapes, colors, and sizes and have different fragrances. Do a little research to find the best rose variety for your container garden.

Primroses

Primroses bloom in early spring and are one of the first flowers you see after winter. This flower will bloom again in the fall and is a great container plant. You can choose between pink, red, blue, yellow, or purple flower varieties, and they come in many shades of each color. Most flowers have a bright yellow center. This flower will bloom twice a year and keep your container garden looking beautiful.

Sunflowers

Sunflowers may grow to a height of ten feet, but they can still be grown in a container. These need a lot of sunlight, so keep them under the full sun. If they bend while trying to reach for the light, they may topple your container over. These beautiful, bright flowers attract wildlife. The flower head has a floret pattern, and this is where you get seeds. Sunflowers are a beautiful focal point for any container garden. Instead of growing them indoors, grow them outside, on an open deck, or in large window boxes.

Zinnias

Zinnias attract butterflies and are beautiful flowers in red, yellow, orange, white, purple, and light green. There are many species of this plant, but Z. elegans is the most commonly grown one. They have different petal arrangements since some flowers have a single row of petals while others might have multiple rows, giving the flower a fuller shape.

Tulips

Tulips can grow to a height of twelve inches and are a sweet-smelling flower that blooms in early spring. They come in different colors like red, pink, orange, purple, yellow, or red-orange. Cold temperatures are important for the tulips can bloom. They thrive in places with this kind of weather and are great for container gardens. This plant can easily survive freezing temperatures and frost.

There are many other flowers that you can explore if you want. The ones mentioned above are the easiest to begin with in a container garden. The more experience you gain, the easier it gets to grow the most beautiful flowers.

Choosing and Combining Container Garden Plants

There are no hard-and-fast rules for designing a container garden. Use your creativity, but remember to provide the plants with what they require for optimum growth. You can apply the following suggestions to create more effective and simple container garden designs.

Create Balance and Contrast

Contrast and balance are the first things to keep in mind.

- The plants and pots must be chosen according to their size. If you use a large pot for a very small plant, it will look lost. Similarly, if you plant a large plant in a very small pot, it will either topple over or just look messy.

- Choose plants that will not grow beyond a height that is double the pot height.

- For simple pots, choose flamboyant plants. For ornate pots, plant something simple; these will complement each other.

- Either plant a single plant in one pot or choose one that adds height, a trailing plant, and a filler to grow together.

Growing a single plant in one container is often the easiest and most balanced option. Instead of growing multiple plants in one pot, try different grouping pots together to create an arrangement.

Color Matters

One of the primary factors to consider is color.

- The colors of your plants should suit the spot you will be growing them in.

- Choose contrasting colors if you want to make a statement.

- If you want to emphasize harmony, choose the same color in different shades. For instance, lavender, purple, and lilac will achieve this effect.

- If you want to accentuate the color of your container, avoid growing a trailing plant that will conceal it.

- Foliage can be used to add color as well.

Focal Points

Consider having a focal point in your container garden to blend in with your aesthetic. Container gardens are a great way to try new things. You can also cultivate whatever type of plant you wish. Combine trees, perennials, vegetables, herbs, and shrubs. If a container strikes your eye when seeking for a focal point, purchase it for your garden. You can always drill some drainage holes in unconventional container options, such as a whiskey barrel. Place your containers in any available open space, such as your deck or patio. It could be outside or inside your home. Use your bamboo or evergreens to create a screen or border for a beautiful added effect. As you continue to do this, you will learn what you like and what you do not. The best thing about containers is how simply they can be relocated. You can disassemble your arrangement and start over whenever you wish.

- Foliage can function as the bones of your garden. The size, color, and texture of the leaves are interesting. For instance, you can use hostas if you want textured, bold leaves, while coleus adds color.

- A focal point can be created by grouping containers, where one large plant is the focus.

- Another way to create a focal point in a container with multiple plants is to choose one strikingly colorful plant.

Tall Focal Points

If you do not add tall plants to your container garden, it can all look too one-dimensional. Many tall plants grow well in pots, so you don't have to opt for the spiky Dracena every time. Just make sure that you grow them in the right-sized pot. Consider using the following as a tall focal point:

- Bougainvillea
- Agave

- Hibiscus

- Common boxwood

- Monterey cypress

- Elephant Ear

Filler Plants

Filler plants make all the difference in a well-designed garden. While the name "filler" may make it appear insignificant, these plants can have an impact on the overall appearance of your container garden. You must take care of them if you want them to grow well and complement the focal point of your garden for a long period. The foliage is an important factor to consider when selecting a filler plant. Growing anything with texture or color will provide visual appeal throughout the season. Consider these filler plants:

- Basil

- Coleus

- Agastache foeniculum

- Celosia

- Fuchsia

- Senecio cineraria

- Lantana

- Swiss chard

Trailing Plants

When you add a trailing plant to your container, it softens and unifies it. There are many fantastic options for you to choose from these days when it comes to trailing plants. Choose a trailer that will bloom for an extended period and not require deadheading anytime soon. Some annuals thrive in hot temperatures, while others thrive in cool weather.

Choose two of these trailers that can be swapped out when the seasons change. Popular trailing plants include:

- Asarina
- Alyssum
- Bidens
- Creeping Zinnia
- Calibrachoa
- Verbena
- Scaevola
- Lotus berthelotii
- Ivy geranium

Tips for Budget-Friendly Container Flower Gardening

Gardening is fun, but it should not cost you more than you can afford. These tips will help you save a few bucks while you try to grow a beautiful container garden.

1. *Trade seeds.* If you know someone who gardens, trade seeds with them. This way, you can grow new plants with someone else's seeds, and they can do the same without any money being wasted on either side. You can also look out for seed swapping events on forums or simply go say "Hi" to a fellow gardener nearby.

2. *Look out for freebies.* Look for listings on sites like Craigslist or Freecycle for freebies. Sometimes landscapers or people moving to different cities put postings where they give away extra plants, scrap wood, or pavers they want to offload. It is an easy score, and all you have to do is go pick it up.

3. *Share cuttings.* If someone shows interest in your plants, share a cutting with them. This way, they will be more likely to let you get cuttings from their garden as well. Many such plants can easily be propagated.

4. *Use bone meal for fertilizer.* The next time you eat some chicken, keep the bones. Clean out any meat or fat that is left over. Then bake the bones in your oven for a couple of hours at 284 degrees. Once the bones are brittle, break them into tiny pieces with a hammer. Remember to wear some safety goggles as they might splinter around. Grind these bits manually using a pestle and mortar and use the powder as fertilizer. It is quite nourishing for your plants.

5. *Utilize takeout containers.* The next time you order takeout or buy instant noodle cups, wash them and make a few holes at the bottom. You can use these to start germinating your seeds before you move them to bigger pots. This way, you save money on having to buy small pots.

6. *Use a plastic jug as a watering can.* Once you finish your milk or orange juice, wash the container with soap and hot water. Make some holes in the cap and use the jug as your watering can. It is easy to carry around, and the size is usually perfect for watering containers.

7. *Paint your trash cans.* Large and fancy planters can be extremely expensive if you want to grow a large plant, but you can use trash cans instead. Just get some basic trashcans and paint them to get the look you want. They look pretty good, serve their purpose, and save you a lot of money.

8. *Replant vegetable scraps.* Green onions, lettuce, and celery are some kitchen greens that you can plant in your containers. Instead of throwing scraps away, put them in some water or a pot of soil.

Other plants that can be grown in this way include mushrooms, onions, and avocados.

9. *Water during cooler hours.* If you want to save on water, switch your watering schedule to the morning or evening. In the afternoon, the heat will cause the water to evaporate faster, which means you will have to water more. In cooler temperatures, the water will not evaporate as fast, and you will not need as much water.

Chapter 11: Common Container Gardening Mistakes

Mistakes happen whether you are a beginner or an experienced gardener. And although we learn most from our mistakes, learning from the mistakes of others never hurts. This chapter will examine common mistakes made by gardeners who experiment with container gardening.

Using the Wrong Containers

Most people do not make holes in pots, and this is where it becomes a problem. One of the most important things about growing plants is to use containers that can drain water out easily, ensuring your plants do not become waterlogged and rot. Containers come with drain holes, but make them if you do not have them. Drill a tiny hole at the bottom of the pot if you need to.

Another mistake people make is using small pots, but these are only good for the little plants you can keep inside your house. It is best to avoid using them outdoors because they will dry too quickly when under the sun. Instead, use large containers, preferably twelve-inch containers, to plant outside; the soil will not dry fast in the sun. You can also use hanging baskets. The best thing to do is to transplant the plant from the basket into a large basket.

Using Heavy Containers

Some people choose to use heavy containers in their garden, and they try moving them after filling them with soil. This is extremely heavy, and if you have just watered it, it will be just that more difficult to move. When you fill and plant any container, large or small, ensure you do it close to its final position. Alternatively, you can place these pots on wheels and then push them around the garden.

Potting Plants Which Do Not Have the Same Requirements

It is important to choose plants that work well together if you want your container garden to thrive. Select plants with the same requirements for soil, fertilizer, sunlight, and moisture. Also, be sure to research before you buy seeds. Read the labels and packets to understand what your plant needs and what to avoid.

Another mistake people make is to plant seeds that have different growth rates next to each other. This is where your experience kicks in. Bear in mind that you cannot expect all plants to grow at the same rate, no matter how healthy they may be. Some may grow an inch in just one day, while others may take longer to grow. If you do plant annual flowers together, they will grow every season at an average rate. These plants do not exceed their space, either.

When you grow plants in the same container, they will receive the same water and sunlight. Thus, always pair plants that require similar conditions. The first thing to do is select plants that can thrive on the amount of sunlight you can provide. For instance, if you have a balcony or patio that faces the south, you know there will be no shade, so you need to choose plants that require a lot of sunlight. Read the labels of every seed you want to buy and match them with the plants that require similar amounts of sunlight.

If you want all of your plants to grow at the same rate, select varieties that grow similarly. You can simply accomplish this by selecting a plant with a variety of colorful blossoms. For instance, you can grow three different colors of calibrachoa in a single pot. To learn how to care for the plant, read the description on the package. If the label indicates that the plant develops quickly or is a vigorous plant, pair it with other plants with similar traits.

You can plant sweet alyssum and supertunia vista bubblegum since they grow well together. They are vigorous plants and require the same amount of water and sunlight.

Not Feeding Your Plants Enough

If you use a potting mix for your container plants, know they contain a few nutrients. Since your plants absorb these nutrients quickly, you need to replace the nutrient content in the soil. Bear in mind that the nutrients in the soil may also get leeched out when you water the plants. If you want to feed your plants well, provide them with enough organic matter.

There are numerous fertilizer products to choose from online or even at the local market. Ensure you choose the right product for your plant. For instance, most flowering plants have different needs when compared to herbs, shrubs, and vegetables. If you want to nourish your plants, use fertilizer regularly. Begin with a slow-release fertilizer and mix that with your potting soil. You should apply a liquid or diluted fertilizer to your plants throughout the growing season. Make sure to apply this twice a month. All-natural or organic fertilizer is the best option as it breaks down and does not cause the buildup of salts or chemicals in the containers.

If you want your flowers to bloom and grow prolifically, feed them consistently. You need to give your plants exactly what they need, and to do this, mix plant food into the potting soil when you begin planting the seeds. Additionally, if you want your plants to grow well, feed them at the right time. Feed your plants regularly, and every time you water them, use plant food that dissolves in water so that it moves to the roots. If you have underused fertilizers in the past, try using some the next time you grow a plant—you will see a difference.

Watering Your Plants Too Much

If you want to avoid overwatering your plants, ensure you have pots with drain holes. This ensures the water drains from the pot. If you use very large containers, drain extra holes in the container. It is essential to understand that your plant may have different moisture requirements. Some plants require water constantly, while others need to be left to dry between watering. Ensure the containers you use drain water quickly.

Before you water any plant, check the soil texture. Put your finger into the soil and check if it is moist. If your fingertip is dry when you pull it out, it means your plant needs to be watered. If you overwater your plants, the leaves will droop, and the plant may turn yellow. Your plants will look limp and wilted. If this is the case, remove the plant from the soil, and replace it with a fresh one. If the soil is very wet, but your plant is still healthy, move the plant into a different container. Alternatively, you can move the plant to a different area where it gets enough wind and sunlight. Wait until the soil dries before you water it again.

Not Watering Your Plants Enough

If you have a container garden at home, it should be watered only once a day. You may need to water the plant for longer in the summer. It is best to water plants in the morning so that they stay hydrated throughout the day. The foliage must have enough time to dry. Most containers, especially small containers, hanging baskets, or window boxes, will need to be watered frequently. You need to do this because the soil will not hold enough moisture.

When watering the plant, make sure to wet it enough so that the water soaks into the soil. Only when this occurs do the minerals and nutrients reach the root. Pour water until you notice it draining.

Some gardeners use synthetic water crystals when they pot their plants. These crystals absorb the water and slowly release it when the soil feels dry. These crystals are expensive, and they do not necessarily maintain much moisture. So, use them only when you know you will not be able to do the watering yourself or when you are leaving your plants unattended for a few days. If your plants dry out, do not despair—even a limp plant can grow well if you give it enough water.

If you use a small container, put it into a bucket and let it fill up with water. If you have a large container, poke holes in the soil so the water reaches the plant roots. Water every plant generously.

Not Following the Correct Plant to Pot Ratio

It is important to consider the proportion of the container size and the plant you want to grow. If you fill a large container with short plants, the plants will appear stunted because they are not in the right pot. A rule of thumb is to have one plant that grows at least as tall as the container. Fill the pot with smaller plants to act as fillers. If you want to balance the look and feel of the pot, add vining or low-growing plants. These will spill over the container's sides, thereby softening the edges of the pot. This is termed the spiller, thriller, and filler.

Never overcrowd the pots you use. These small plants will increase in number during their growing season. If you use small containers, ensure you plant small plants only.

Buying Weak, Sick Plants

It is crucial to purchase plants from the right nursery, which is the best way to start. You should do this if you want to grow healthy plants at home. If you purchase your plant from a local nursery, you can purchase pest-free, disease-free, and well-cared-for plants. If you go to a local nursery, you will learn everything there is to know about the plant you are buying. The staff will have the information you need to have a good yield. Ask them everything you want to know about the plant. This is the only way to ensure you have a healthy and suitable plant at home.

If you purchase plants at large stores, you may bring home diseased plants. This is a little risky since large distributors may not care for their produce as much as your local mom-and-pop store. If you cannot resist doing this, ensure you purchase the plant from the distributor when they are being delivered at the store. Speak to an employee who knows when the new stock comes in and buy the plants then.

Write down where you bought plants from. For example, if you buy a plant infected with pests, remove the plant from around other plants, along with other plants you bought from the same vendor. This is to ensure the other plants are not affected by the pest infestation.

Not Pruning Your Plants

When your plants become spindly, leggy, or sparse, prune them. You can cut or shear them if you are comfortable doing so. Then, move the plant to a different spot until the plant begins to grow well again. Cut or prune frequently, so it grows happily.

Living with Dying Plants

You may have tried everything conceivable with your plant, yet it still appears to be in poor condition. If the plant does not improve, simply toss it into your compost pile. If you do not have a pile, toss the plant in the garbage; if the plant is unhealthy, burn it and dispose of the soil. It is best to start over in case the disease spreads to other plants.

Setting the Wrong Expectations

When you choose to set up a container garden, you need to design the garden. Evaluate the time you will spend setting up the garden and whether you have the time to maintain and care for the garden. If you travel a lot, you need to choose the right irrigating system or self-watering containers. Alternatively, you can ask someone close to your house to care for your plants so they are healthy when you are away. You can also buy plants that do not require too much water.

Your garden reflects your way of life. Do you like a formal or a casual way of life? Do you enjoy planning, or do you prefer random arrangements? Some people prefer containers that are formal, neat, and well planned. Others do not mind if their plants grow for miles; the focus is solely on color and not on design.

Using Filler Material to Cover the Bottom of Large Containers

The Internet is filled with different ideas you can use to fill up your containers. You may have come across various websites where people have suggested that you use pot shards or old shoes to fill the base of your large container. This is a terrible idea. Your plants need soil and nutrients to grow. Your container can be sixteen inches deep or six inches deep, but this does not matter when it comes to your plants. You need to fill it with potting soil. If you use filler material at the bottom of the container, it can cause water accumulation. This will ultimately lead to the rotting of roots. You need to have good-quality potting soil in the containers. This soil drains easily and is lightweight, and this is what your plant needs to survive.

Not Using Potting Soil

This is another mistake some people make. They use garden soil instead of potting soil. It is difficult to differentiate between the two just by looking at them. If you are at the store, look for a bag that says potting soil. This bag will be lighter when compared to gardening soil. Potting soil of high quality does not contain soil but rather a mix of materials, such as perlite, bark, and peat moss. These materials ensure your plant has enough air and that water drains easily.

Not Watering the Roots

Some people water only the foliage and not the roots. This is where the problem lies. You need to point your watering can or spray toward the end of the container. Do not worry about watering the foliage or spraying the flowers and leaves because that is not very important—it only wastes water and can lead to other diseases in the future. Bear in mind that your roots need water. The top of your plant will get water from the roots.

Leaving Your Plants Unchecked

From earlier, you know that all plants do not grow at the same pace, and you may choose some plants that don't grow well in containers. Some may grow exceptionally well when compared to others. Some plants may be more robust when compared to others. If the plants that grow vigorously are not checked, they may overtake the other plants and suck up the nutrition. It is okay for you to prune and trim the plants and ensure they do not grow out of proportion or get too big. Ensure you do not remove more than twenty percent of any plant at any point in time.

Container gardens are a great way to improve the way your garden looks. There is much room for error, but there is a lot of room for experimentation. If you select plants that complement and work well with each other, then you do not have to worry about your garden. It is best to try different colors and combinations that match your sense of style. Choose a container garden design that works best for you.

Ensure you choose the suitable soil for your plants and the right seeds. It is also important to evenly space the seeds so that the plants have enough space to grow. Keep these mistakes in mind and try to avoid them. Keep the tips mentioned in this chapter in mind to ensure your plants grow well.

Conclusion

Gardening is one of the most fun, healthy, and useful activities to take part in. The more time you spend gardening, the more you realize how addictive and therapeutic it is. In addition, you get to grow your own food and flowers, all while having a lot of much-needed fun. Use this book to get started with your container garden, and remember to be consistent. Gardening is not just about planting a seed and watering it—as you well know by now. It requires regular care and maintenance, but your efforts will definitely pay off. And the satisfaction of seeing your plants thrive is unparalleled.

To begin, select some low-maintenance plants and then progress to others. Choose the vegetables or herbs that you consume the most if you wish to grow your food. Do your research so that you can properly care for the plants. Then, proper watering, fertilizing, mulching, and so on will help it flourish. Plants, like humans, require nutrition and must be protected from pests and diseases. Take care of your garden, and it will reward you in more ways than one.

Bear in mind that you are going to make mistakes. This is especially true for beginners—although experienced gardeners can slip up now and then. Read the labels well and identify the right plants for your garden.

Keep the tips outlined by this book in mind when you sow seeds. Do not beat yourself up if you make mistakes; instead, learn from them.

As you gain experience, you can have fun with the aesthetics of your container garden. Choose fun pots and paint them in different colors, or decorate them in a way that speaks to you. There is a lot you can do with containers! And while you do all that, your love for gardening will continue to grow and bear fruit. This book will be your reference whenever you need it, but for now, just go out there and start gardening!

Here's another book by Dion Rosser that you might like

Bibliography

Albert, Steve. "Pot and Container Sizes for Growing Vegetable Crops." Harvest to Table. November 15, 2015. https://harvesttotable.com/pot-and-container-sizes-for-growing-vegetable-crops/

BalconyContainerGardening.com. "25 Flowers for Container Gardens." Accessed July 1, 2021. http://www.balconycontainergardening.com/plants/406-flowers

Beaty, Vanessa. "The 35 Easiest Container and Pot Friendly Fruits, Vegetables and Herbs." DIY & Crafts. July 7, 2014. https://www.diyncrafts.com/7137/food/35-easiest-container-pot-friendly-fruit-vegetables-herbs

Beck, Andrea. "13 Herbs to Fill Your Container Gardens with Fresh Flavors and Scents." Better Homes & Gardens. June 9, 2021. https://www.bhg.com/gardening/vegetable/herbs/best-herbs-for-container-gardens/

Enjoy Container Gardening. "Pests in Container Gardens." Accessed July 1, 2021. https://www.enjoycontainergardening.com/blog/pests-in-container-gardens/

Foote, Natasha. "11 of the Best Vegetables to Grow in Pots and Containers." Gardener's Path. August 24, 2019. https://gardenerspath.com/plants/vegetables/best-container/

Garden Mentors. "How to Prepare Containers for Planting." May 14, 2021. https://gardenmentors.com/garden-help/gardening-guidelines/how-to-prepare-containers-for-planting/

HGTV. "Easiest Vegetables to Grow in Flower Pots." Accessed July 1, 2021. https://www.hgtv.com/outdoors/flowers-and-plants/vegetables/easiest-vegetables-grow-flower-pot-pictures

Iannotti, Marie. "Choosing and Combining Plants for Container Gardens." The Spruce. June 20, 2018. https://www.thespruce.com/choosing-And-combining-plants-for-container-gardens-1402062

Jabbour, Niki. "The 7 best herbs for container gardening." Savvy Gardening. June 29, 2017. https://savvygardening.com/best-herbs-for-container-gardening/

Jimerson, Doug. "11 Easy Colorful Container Garden Ideas." Costa Farms. Accessed July 1, 2021. http://www.costafarms.com/get-growing/slideshow/11-easy-colorful-container-garden-ideas

Marken, Bill, & DeJohn, Suzanne. "Common Plant Diseases in Container Gardens." Dummies. Accessed July 1, 2021. https://www.dummies.com/home-garden/gardening/container-gardening/common-plant-diseases-in-container-gardens/

Martin, Susan. "10 Container Gardening Mistakes to Avoid." Proven Winners. Accessed July 1, 2021. https://www.provenwinners.com/learn/top-ten-lists/10-container-gardening-mistakes-avoid

Michaels, Kerry. "6 Tips for Growing Fruit Trees in Containers." The Spruce. November 2, 2019. https://www.thespruce.com/growing-fruit-trees-in-containers-848164

Michaels, Kerry. "Easy Tips for Growing Herbs in Containers." The Spruce. February 10, 2021. https://www.thespruce.com/growing-herbs-in-pots-getting-started-3876523

Michaels, Kerry. "10 Common Container Gardening Mistakes." The Spruce. April 15, 2021. https://www.thespruce.com/common-container-gardening-mistakes-847796

Michaels, Kerry. "10 Best Vegetables That Grow in Containers." The Spruce. June 8, 2021. https://www.thespruce.com/great-vegetables-to-grow-in-containers-848214

Trimble, Derek. "How to Prepare Flower Pots for Planting." Accessed July 1, 2021. https://www.hgtv.com/outdoors/landscaping-and-hardscaping/preparing-your-pots-for-planting-pictures

Tukua, Deborah. "22 Ways to Combat Garden Pests Naturally." Farmers' Almanac. May 3, 2019. https://www.farmersalmanac.com/combat-garden-pests-naturally-20886

Carruthers, W. B. (2020, April 29). Greenhouse Tools & Equipment. Cultivargreenhouses.Co.Uk. https://www.cultivargreenhouses.co.uk/inspiration/greenhouse-tools-equipment

Ellis, M. E. (2017, December 19). Pros and cons of growing in A greenhouse - gardening know-how's blog. Gardeningknowhow.Com. https://blog.gardeningknowhow.com/gardening-pros-cons/pros-and-cons-of-growing-in-a-greenhouse/

Gardening - Feeding: fertilizing and watering. (n.d.). In Encyclopedia Britannica.

The greenhouse gardening guide. (2011, March 31). Proflowers.Com. https://www.proflowers.com/blog/greenhouse-gardening-guide

Weasel, G. (2014, July 15). Greenhouses: Pros & cons - garden weasel. Gardenweasel.Com. https://www.gardenweasel.com/greenhouses-pros-cons/

What garden tools are best in a greenhouse? (2018, June 22). Hartley-Botanic.Com. https://hartley-botanic.com/magazine/garden-tools-best-greenhouse/

Ana, M. (2018, April 25). Cheap and sturdy greenhouse foundation options [2020]. Growingreenhouse.Com. https://www.growingreenhouse.com/greenhouse-foundation-options/

Can you use pressure-treated wood in a greenhouse? (n.d.). Askinglot.Com. Retrieved from https://askinglot.com/can-you-use-pressure-treated-wood-in-a-greenhouse

Carruthers, W. B. (2020, May 13). How to build a greenhouse base. Cultivargreenhouses.Co.Uk. https://www.cultivargreenhouses.co.uk/inspiration/building-a-greenhouse-base

Greenhouse Knowledge Hub. (n.d.). Greenhousesdirect.Co.Uk. Retrieved from https://www.greenhousesdirect.co.uk/help-advice/base-requirements/

Preparing the base for your greenhouse. (n.d.). Greenhousepeople.Co.Uk. Retrieved from https://www.greenhousepeople.co.uk/pages/100/5-buyers-guide-preparing-your-base/

All you need to know about greenhouse foundation & flooring. (2020, May 19). Greenhouseemporium.Com. https://greenhouseemporium.com/blogs/greenhouse-gardening/greenhouse-foundation/

Ana, M. (2017, November 27). 5 greenhouse frame materials: What's the best one? Growingreenhouse.Com. https://www.growingreenhouse.com/greenhouse-frame-material/

Ana, M. (2018, April 25). Cheap and sturdy greenhouse foundation options [2020]. Growingreenhouse.Com. https://www.growingreenhouse.com/greenhouse-foundation-options/

Greenhouse Kits and greenhouse and garden supplies. (n.d.). Greenhousecatalog.Com. Retrieved from https://www.greenhousecatalog.com/greenhouse-frame

How to build a DIY greenhouse. (n.d.). Blackanddecker.Com. from https://www.blackanddecker.com/ideas-and-inspiration/projects/greenhouse-how-to

Creating A greenhouse: What are your best window options? (2016, January 29). Clerawindows.Com. https://www.clerawindows.com/blog/creating-a-greenhouse-what-are-your-best-window-options/

FAQs - Hartley Botanic. (n.d.). Hartley-Botanic.Com. Retrieved from https://hartley-botanic.com/help-and-support/faqs/

How do I Choose the Best Greenhouse Windows? (n.d.). Homequestionsanswered.Com. Retrieved from https://www.homequestionsanswered.com/how-do-i-choose-the-best-greenhouse-windows.htm

The BEST GREENHOUSE DOOR (DIY) build. (2019, April 4).

Which is the best choice for greenhouse panels? - tuflite. (2016, May 26). Tuflite.Com. https://www.tuflite.com/blog/best-choice-greenhouse-panels

Greenhouse Irrigation - What's the best watering system? (2021, April 9). Greenhouseemporium.Com. https://greenhouseemporium.com/blogs/greenhouse-gardening/greenhouse-irrigation-systems/

Complete guide about Greenhouse Irrigation System. (2019, August 7). Automatworld.In. https://www.automatworld.in/blog/greenhouse-irrigation-system/

andava. (2019, April 19). Greenhouse temperature considerations - aer industries. Aerindustries.Com. https://aerindustries.com/blog/2019/04/19/greenhouse-temperature/

Esquira, N. (2019, December 29). Optimal humidity and temperature for greenhouse growing - drygair greenhouse dehumidifiers. Drygair.Com. https://drygair.com/what-are-the-optimal-humidity-and-temperature-set-points-for-greenhouse-growing/

Reducing humidity in the greenhouse. (2015, March 6). Umass.Edu. https://ag.umass.edu/greenhouse-floriculture/fact-sheets/reducing-humidity-in-greenhouse

Rusnak, P. (2019, August 9). How to create the ideal ventilation system for your greenhouse. Greenhousegrower.Com. https://www.greenhousegrower.com/technology/how-to-create-the-ideal-ventilation-system-for-your-greenhouse/

Understanding greenhouse lighting. (n.d.). Growspan.Com. Retrieved from https://www.growspan.com/news/understanding-greenhouse-lighting/

Sabeh, N. (2020, June 22). Greenhouse ventilation: natural or mechanical? Greenhouse Management. https://www.greenhousemag.com/article/2020-structures-report-greenhouse-ventilation-natural-or-mechanical/

Wollaeger, H. (2016, November 1). Choose the right light. Greenhouse Management. https://www.greenhousemag.com/article/choose-the-right-light/

Choosing the right lighting for your greenhouse. (n.d.). Ggs-Greenhouse.Com. Retrieved from https://ggs-greenhouse.com/blog/choosing-the-right-lighting-for-your-greenhouse

Heidi Lindberg, Michigan State University Extension. (n.d.). Insecticides for common pests on greenhouse vegetables and transplants - MSU Extension. Msu.Edu. Retrieved from https://www.canr.msu.edu/news/insecticides_for_common_pests_on_greenhouse_vegetables_and_transplants

How to grow a Greenhouse Vegetable Garden. (2012, July 29). Sfgate.Com. https://homeguides.sfgate.com/grow-greenhouse-vegetable-garden-36456.html

Vegetables: growing in your greenhouse. (n.d.). Org.Uk. Retrieved from https://www.rhs.org.uk/advice/profile?PID=613

Ana, M. (2020, March 20). What are the best fruit to grow in A greenhouse? Retrieved from Growingreenhouse.com website: https://www.growingreenhouse.com/what-are-the-best-fruit-to-grow-in-a-greenhouse/

Can I grow fruit trees in a greenhouse? (2020, July 20). Retrieved from Greenhouseemporium.com website: https://greenhouseemporium.com/blogs/greenhouse-gardening/growing-fruit-trees-in-greenhouse/

(N.d.). Retrieved from Permaculturenews.org website: https://www.permaculturenews.org/2019/11/02/how-to-grow-fresh-fruit-all-year-long/

Gilrein, D. (2013, November 25). Big nuisance, tiny pest. Retrieved from Greenhouse Management website: https://www.greenhousemag.com/article/gm1213-managing-shore-flies/

Waterworth, K. (2013, December 7). Greenhouse pest control - pest management in greenhouses. Retrieved from Gardeningknowhow.com website:

https://www.gardeningknowhow.com/special/greenhouses/greenhouse-plant-pests.htm

Baley, A. (2013, October 11). Greenhouse herb gardening - using A greenhouse for growing herbs. Gardeningknowhow.Com. https://www.gardeningknowhow.com/special/greenhouses/growing-greenhouse-herbs.htm

Contributor, H. (2020, October 27). Growing herbs in a greenhouse: What you need to know. Happysprout.Com; HappySprout. https://www.happysprout.com/indoor-plants/herbs-greenhouse-growing/

gardeningchannel. (2021, February 26). 16 best herbs to grow in your home greenhouse. Gardeningchannel.Com. https://www.gardeningchannel.com/top-herbs-home-greenhouse/

Grant, A. (2013, December 1). Troubleshooting the herb garden - protecting herb gardens from pests and diseases. Gardeningknowhow.Com. https://www.gardeningknowhow.com/edible/herbs/hgen/herb-growing-problems.htm

Pest control and herbs - greenhouse product news. (2003, April 22). Gpnmag.Com. https://gpnmag.com/article/pest-control-and-herbs/

Ten mistakes new herb gardeners make (and how to avoid them). (2014, April 7). Heeman.Ca. https://heeman.ca/garden-guides/10-herb-gardening-mistakes/

Vinje, E. (2012, December 8). How to grow herbs. Planetnatural.Com. https://www.planetnatural.com/herb-gardening/

42 easy to grow greenhouse plants for beginners. (2019, April 12). Greenhouseemporium.Com. https://greenhouseemporium.com/blogs/greenhouse-gardening/easy-to-grow-greenhouse-plant/

A guide to using pots, tubs, and window boxes. (n.d.). Lovethegarden.Com. Retrieved from https://www.lovethegarden.com/uk-en/article/guide-using-pots-tubs-and-window-boxes

Alexander, C. (2018, November 28). A greenhouse Winter Garden - FineGardening. Finegardening.Com. https://www.finegardening.com/article/a-greenhouse-winter-garden

Ana, M. (2020, May 12). 50 plants to grow in A greenhouse (with pictures)! Growingreenhouse.Com. https://www.growingreenhouse.com/50-plants-to-grow-in-a-greenhouse-with-pictures/

Greenhouse pest control: Top 10 tips. (2016, January 22). Primrose.Co.Uk. https://blog.primrose.co.uk/2016/01/greenhouse-pest-control-top-10-tips/

Middleton, K. (2021, April 22). 5 best plants to grow in your greenhouse. Gardenbuildingsdirect.Co.Uk. https://www.gardenbuildingsdirect.co.uk/blog/best-greenhouse-plants-to-grow/

Miller, L. (2020, March 6). Slatted box container growing – putting plants in A wooden crate. Gardeningknowhow.Com. https://www.gardeningknowhow.com/special/containers/growing-plants-in-wooden-crates.htm

Vinje, E. (2012, December 10). How to plant in pots - container gardening. Planetnatural.Com. https://www.planetnatural.com/container-gardening/

Waterworth, K. (2013, October 9). Growing plants in A greenhouse - suitable plants for greenhouse gardening. Gardeningknowhow.Com. https://www.gardeningknowhow.com/special/greenhouses/plants-for-greenhouses.htm

Why do plants grow better in a greenhouse? (2019, December 16). Hartley-Botanic.Com. https://hartley-botanic.com/magazine/plants-grow-better-greenhouse/

(N.d.). Themicrogardener.Com. Retrieved from https://themicrogardener.com/choosing-a-container-the-pros-and-cons-2/

Year-round greenhouse planting calendar. (n.d.). Ceresgs.Com. Retrieved from https://ceresgs.com/year-round-greenhouse-planting-calendar/

Ebert, J. (2020, December 27). Gardening calendar 2021 – what to grow in your greenhouse each month. Homes & Gardens. https://www.homesandgardens.com/news/gardening-calendar

Planting Calendar. (n.d.). Tuigarden.Co.Nz. Retrieved from https://tuigarden.co.nz/planting-calendar

Printed in Dunstable, United Kingdom

76046923R00167